QUEENDOM

The Ultimate Guide to a Female Led Relationship

MARISA RUDDER

All of Marisa Rudder's Bestselling Books are available on Amazon:

Love & Obey, Real Men Worship Women, Oral Sex for Women, Cuckolding, Spanking, Chastity, Turning Point, and *Swinging.*

Please contact Marisa Rudder with any questions: Email: femaleledrelationshipbook@gmail.com

Printed in the United States of America Publisher's Cataloging-in- Publication data

ISBN: 978-1-7361835-4-0

Author of *Love & Obey, Real Men Worship Women, Oral Sex for Women, Cuckolding, Spanking, Chastity,* and *Turning Point*

DEDICATION

I want to thank everyone who has supported me throughout the unfolding of this incredible vision of the *Love & Obey* movement. To all those who purchased and read each one of my books and followed my social media for the last four years, I offer my eternal gratitude. You inspired me to push for more female empowerment, sexual freedom, and the betterment of relationships and marriage. I could not have accomplished all that I have without your encouragement and support.

Thank you all for everything you do for me. I love you all and dedicate this book to those men and women who have faithfully followed my guidance and take time out to include me in your journey. You are all so wonderful and so kind. Thank you for believing in this cause, which has already changed thousands of lives. My goal is to continue to fight for change. Men and women deserve to be happy in their lives and be in the relationships they desire. The future is female led, and the *Love & Obey* Movement where supportive men worship their women as Queens will prevail.

Available on Amazon Books.

Please contact: Marisa Rudder

Email: femaleledrelationshipbook@gmail.com

Printed in the United States of America Publisher's Cataloging-in-

Publication data

ISBN: 978-1-7361835-4-0

You can find out more about the *Love & Obey* Female Led Lifestyle and all my books on my website:

www.loveandobey.com

Or follow me on social media:

FACEBOOK

https://www.facebook.com/femaleledrelationships

TWITTER

https://twitter.com/loveandobeybook

INSTAGRAM

https://www.instagram.com/femaleledrelationships

YOUTUBE

https://www.youtube.com/channel/UCkX3wmd934WR1 03hStbzbiQ?view_as=subscriber

Introduction

Queendom is the new kingdom. A territory ruled over by a monarch who is a woman. For centuries everyone worked for or was part of the kingdom. The kingdom, which was ruled by a monarch, was a symbol of inspiration, unity, and stability. People devoted their lives to serving their ruler, and they were contributors to the existence and survival of the kingdom.

Today, the kingdom is being replaced by the Queendom. The British Royal Family is a great example of this. The Queen has ruled for almost 100 years and shows no signs of slowing down. The females in the Royal family commanded attention from Princess Margaret to Princess Diana, and now, her royal highness Kate Middleton, soon to be Queen. Now you and your Queen can create your own Queendom where your Queen rules over the household, and you are her supportive gentleman. You will treat her like the ruling monarch over your household, which is now your Queendom, as it is ruled by the Queen.

Today, men and women are enjoying the freedom to run their relationships the way they choose, and more women are naturally taking charge in marriages and relationships. Couples are experiencing a deeper connection and passionate love. The interesting thing about love is you cannot own it or control it, but it can own you. Have you ever felt a love that consumed you, overwhelmed you, made you feel like you could literally go out of your mind? That's the love in a Queendom and in the Female Led Relationship (FLR). It's a love that you never experience in any other type of relationship because when your Queen exerts her power and dominance over you and you freely submit to her as the supportive gentleman, you form a bond that becomes almost unbreakable, and you feel a love that is more intense than any other.

Female Led Relationships are growing, and couples are enjoying more happiness, excitement, and increased sexual satisfaction. Today, women are leading in countries, governments, corporations, and now, relationships. In 2021, Kamala Harris made history as the first female Vice President of the United States, the NFL hired the first female referee who participated in the Super Bowl, and baseball hired its first female General Manager.

In the Olympics, women dominated and accounted for almost 50 percent of all participants. Surfing became an Olympic sport and a woman from the USA was the first to claim the gold medal. Jeff Bezos, founder of Amazon, chose a woman, who was one of the first female astronauts decades ago, to accompany him on his first venture into space. There are many more examples of females breaking the glass ceiling and entering areas previously dominated by men.

I experienced the challenge of entering a male-dominated field as an engineering student years ago, and as the creator of the *Love & Obey* Movement, I have not only been a participant, but I have been a witness to the rise of female empowerment, and there are no signs of this slowing down. It is only natural that now, women should take their rightful place as a leader at home and in the bedroom as well. Men are loving this transition because it means they can occupy an appropriate role as supportive gentlemen.

Leopold von Sacher-Masoch said, "Man is the one who desires, woman the one who is desired. This is the woman's entire but decisive advantage." For centuries, the head of the Queen's Army has been a strong leader, and he still answers to the Queen. Modern-day British royalty is a perfect example of a matriarchy run by the Queen. One in which all men, even her late husband, had to be completely submissive to her rule. But Female Led Relationships are becoming more common.

There is a new era of female dominance, occupied by well-educated, ambitious women, and they are shaping the future of the world. We live in a transitional era when women are becoming the dominant force within our society, and men are learning to be obedient, happy, and submit to female loving authority. In a Female Led Relationship, a woman takes the lead, and she is the dominant partner, while a man serves her as the submissive one. She makes all the important decisions and has more authority than the man. A Female Led Relationship often occurs out of a desire for a strong woman to lead while the man is content being a supportive gentleman.

While this seems like the opposite of what we have been taught, it has been this way for centuries. Since prehistoric times, the man went out and did the hunting and the work while the woman stayed at home with the family. While this was used to condition society to believe that men are stronger and women are weaker; therefore, the man should have the control. This patriarchal conditioning was used to cement a woman's role for decades as subservient, but I see it as the opposite. Within the family unit, the Queen has always been the most important part of life, so when a woman is in charge of what is essentially crucial to life, that raises her level above a man. In addition, a man went out and served his woman by hunting and bringing home food. Hence, bringing home the "bacon."

Most researchers are unsure of exactly when men were placed in charge while women had to be subservient. Many agree that much of it was patriarchal conditioning occurring because of the church and laws, which were enacted to prevent women from owning property. It was both the pervasive idea that women were second to men and withholding of basic rights like voting, owning property, and occupying key positions in the workforce which contributed to women being subservient. However, times are changing. Today, a woman can not only be in charge of her life, work, and the household, she now holds the reins in the marriage or relationship.

Women in leadership are becoming more common worldwide, and they are now rising to take the lead in many industries, companies, and at home. This book will give you the tools you need to be a great lover and be a great servant to your Goddess. It will change the way you approach your relationship daily, because by fully satisfying your queen, you place her on a pedestal and become her support system so she can feel empowered and confident to do her job as leader of both your lives and your relationship.

What you will witness is a transformation in the love and passion you experience. Women are changed when they are in a Female Led Relationship. They feel happy, inspired, and loved every day, and you feel accepted, valuable, and special in return because you have created this change in her. There is nothing like a powerful woman who is free to be the queen. This makes you both more loving and freer to be completely honest in your marriage or relationship.

Today millions of women rule over their husbands in Female Led Relationships, whether it is as the primary financial provider or the man is the provider, allowing her to be the Queen. Female Led Relationships are becoming more common with celebrities, athletes, and executives, and they have always been alive and well with the wealthy class. Why? Because strong, powerful men know the value of a strong Queen. How much stronger is the kingdom than when there is a strong, powerful Queen with an equally strong king placing her on a pedestal and allowing her to take charge. This is the basis of a Female Led Relationship. The man is not weak or insignificant. He is the general, the supporting force in the relationship. Women are no longer riding in the passenger seat; they are the drivers. I know many real-life examples of women taking charge of their lives, careers, and relationships, resulting in dramatically changing their men's lives.

The 80s movie called *Romeo Is Bleeding* is a movie that accurately describes how men come under the spell of a powerful woman. It's the story of a police officer and how he loses his mind with loving so many women, including a female assassin who literally turns his life upside down and controls him sexually. This is the power of female domination, and you will lust after your Queen. This gets me thinking about the love that consumes you. What is love without lust? Is it a great friendship you are looking for? Or are you looking for an incredible romantic adventure?

Couples are discovering that something magical happens in a Female Led Relationship. Your attitude and behavior toward each other changes. The woman rises to be Queen, and her inner Goddess emerges. The man becomes a real gentleman who feels his sole purpose is to serve. He is always thinking of his Queen's happiness and desires first.

Couples see their love growing into the kind of love they cannot own or control. *Love & Obey* Female Led Relationship creates the kind of love that owns and controls you. Come along on this adventure of passion that is likely to transform your marriage and relationship from boring and mundane to exciting and exhilarating every single day. Don't you and your Queen deserve a chance to take your journey to a new level of love and adventure?

Table of Contents

CHAPTER 1

What is a Female Led Relationship?

A Female Led Relationship is one where the woman takes the lead and assumes the role of the dominant partner, with men taking the more submissive role. The woman will be in charge of the important decisions and carries more authority in the relationship. There are many reasons why couples decide to get into a Female Led Relationship, and many more are switching from normal marriages and relationships to wife led marriages. I receive thousands of messages from couples making the transition and from men actively seeking a dominant woman. Female led lifestyle is beginning to emerge in media, such as movies and TV shows, with so many great female characters taking charge.

Some of the classics are even changing their formula from male-dominated to female. The very popular James Bond series is a great example of the move from the Agent 007 being the strong, tough lead character to now females taking over for the 2021 release. Wonder Woman was a sensation as a follow-up to Superman, and she is the superior character in *Justice League*. The show *The Equalizer* casts Queen Latifah instead of the usual male character played by Denzel Washington. I believe that with female led growing and the abundance of strong, capable female characters depicted in mainstream media in addition to couples making up 50 percent of the population being raised by single mothers, more men are craving female authority.

Of course, a Female Led Relationship can have challenges, such as deciding on who will manage the money, make the household decisions, and plan social events. Understanding the guidelines of how to exist in this type of relationship is crucial. As it's new, there will always be issues to overcome, but generally, there are fewer power struggles when the leader, the Queen, is established right from the start with the man being the supportive gentleman.

A great example of female led is the Queen head of the British Royal Family. The Queen is the leader, and Prince Philip was her supportive gentleman, a role he fulfilled dutifully till his passing. Prince Philip was a wonderful example of how an alpha male could still be alpha but also accept his role as submissive to his Queen. Many may say it's just tradition, but Prince Philip has said on many occasions that he had to adjust to the role and do a lot of training to be able to succeed.

The same is true for couples in Female Led Relationships. The misconception is that men who agree to be in this type of relationship are naturally submissive or weak. This could not be further from the truth. Some men are submissive and enjoy being with a stronger woman, but there are many alpha men just as eager to serve a powerful woman as his Queen, and they are happy to be the supportive gentleman.

Even in patriarchal times, the only person who could control a man was a woman. There are many examples of how powerful men were brought to their knees, good or bad, by women. Wallace Simpson changed the course of history when King Edward abdicated the throne. King Henry VIII, notorious womanizer, made his mistress Anne Boleyn a queen and went against the church to do it—for a woman. There are even modern-day examples, like Bill Clinton's impeachment due to a woman and Prince Harry marrying a bi-racial common American woman, Megan Markle, and moving away from the monarchy to live their lives in North America—all under a woman's influence.

Women are powerful in many areas, and in the Female Led Relationship, you are submitting to that power. You show your ultimate respect in the bedroom, which was once an area of male dominance, and now becomes a place of female worship. So why does this work so effortlessly? Women have become accustomed to taking charge. In *Gone with the Wind,* I was fascinated when the men went off to war and the women still continued to survive and took charge. In a world where women were expected to follow men, in their absence, females stepped up and managed everything.

Women have a natural ability to lead because they are multi-taskers and great communicators. Women form relationships with other people better than men. They are collaborators, and nothing can get done as an island. Today in 2021, women are finally exercising their natural ability to be the ruler and men as the supporter. Oral sex is part of the supportive man's duties, and in Female Led Relationships, sex is for the Queen's pleasure. How you pleasure your Queen becomes your opportunity to show your Goddess how much you adore her. Your willingness to ensure her happiness will transform your life's purpose. When men discover their new life purpose of loving, obeying, and serving a superior female, they will find peace and contentment. In addition, the loving female authority who rules over him will provide him with tremendous amounts of love and affection.

The general rule implies that when you decide to create a Female Led Relationship, you must both agree that she is in charge. This is of great importance to establish early on to prevent any power struggles later on. There may be additional challenges with men who like the idea of being in a Female Led Relationship but they are unable to fully commit because of previous patriarchal conditioning. My seven books in the *Love and Obey* series help with this transition properly into the lifestyle. It is my hope that this book, which will serve as the ultimate guide to everything female led, will help you to create the perfect Female Led Relationship or female led marriage for you and your Queen. One that will not only be based on the foundation of honesty, trust, and open communication but one that will allow both of you to thrive and be fully satisfied every day of your life.

Women seem to come alive when there are fewer arguments and more constructive support happening in daily life. When you listen to her intently, participate in conversations, and encourage her ideas and goals, you help your Queen become a dynamic, successful person who is inspirational to everyone around you, including your kids. Children mimic their parents, and they need examples of success, maturity, and love to inspire them daily. A woman with a strong supportive man is free to be the shining star she is meant to be, and it leads me to think about the saying, "Behind every great woman is a great man." So, obedience to a woman should never be seen as weakness. Strong men know the tremendous benefits of supporting a strong woman.

Women have felt their power growing each year. For many, "The Future is Female" and "Girl Boss" is the new normal. I began to notice this sharp increase in female empowerment themes in movies, TV shows, YouTube, governments, corporations, and in general households. Everywhere, I have witnessed examples of women taking charge, and now it is becoming a worldwide phenomenon in relationships and society. They embrace the idea of female superiority and leadership.

The support I received from men about reading *Love & Obey* and practicing it daily, and the hundreds of testimonials I received, was overwhelming. Men everywhere tell me how they enjoy and have learned to worship women. Empowering a woman to lead should not be viewed as negative, as it helps to build a stronger, fulfilling relationship. Women are enjoying and welcoming the new role to teach men how to become loving and obedient. I believe that this is the best lifestyle for a truly successful and happy relationship and offers the most opportunity for both people to grow and evolve together.

CHAPTER 2

Why Do Women Like Female Led Relationships?

Why do women love Female Led Relationships ? My answer is: what's there not to love. All of your needs met, a loving, obedient man who puts you on a pedestal and worships you like a Queen every day. I have found that women love Female Led Relationships because they can finally be free to assert their dominance and can step into their rightful role as leaders. Women have always naturally led households and made decisions at home, and this is where it all begins. A properly run household makes a happy, successful family. Children learn most from their homes, and what happens in our homes and family relationships affects us over our entire lifetime.

I can recall the number of times in early relationships when I purposely subdued my dominant, take-charge personality for the sake of my partner. In the beginning, many strong women felt they had to abide by society's patriarchal rules allowing their men to seemingly have control while they maneuvered from being second. However, this eventually causes problems because a female led woman cannot suppress her nature forever.

As I have experienced, at some point, she will be unhappy being submissive when her true nature is to be a leader. Having control over their relationship, household, kids, finances, and everything else, is just a part of a woman's personality. The freedom to lead in a Female Led Relationship allows women to be involved in their rightful role as Queen and prevents them from feeling suppressed.

Female Led Relationships defy the traditional relationship dynamic in which the man has authority over the woman. They also defy traditional gender roles that our patriarchal society has imposed on women, and it gives women a chance to make meaningful decisions, changes, and contributions to their household without having to go through a male's approval first. There is less of a power struggle in a Female Led Relationship, as the roles are clear. The woman can make her decisions peacefully, knowing she has her partner's support. While it is a debated issue, some women feel that an FLR allows them more control of their partner and allows them to change bad habits and help them better themselves.

The advantage of a Female Led Relationship is that it sets clear roles and removes the potential for power struggles. It establishes the proper hierarchy. No one in British Royalty questions who is at the head. The Queen reigns supreme, and everyone in the UK and worldwide show their respect to her. There is a wonderful scene where Churchill visits Queen Elizabeth for the first time, and he is standing while conversing with her for an hour. The Queen is perplexed but later Churchill explained that it was his duty to show respect to her by remaining standing until she would allow him to sit. He wasn't allowed to interrupt her or speak before she spoke. These rules help to establish order, and in a Female Led Relationship, having clear roles in the relationship reduces fights.

Both you and your Queen must be familiar with the rules as they will need to be reinforced constantly, especially in the beginning. As human beings, we tend to fall back into learned behavior, and you will want to act out and maybe speak out of turn to your Queen. You may yell and raise your voice inappropriately, and all of these behaviors must change if the relationship is to run smoothly. My suggestion is to write out the rules and have them be visible to deter arguments.

Long before I began to write about Female Led Relationship, I was pleasantly surprised walking into a friend's house and seeing a board with division of duties and roles clearly written. I was impressed because my friend had not admitted to being in a Female Led Relationship, yet she had taken the responsibility of utilizing some of the tools. By defining clearly the roles and duties for her and her husband, there were rarely any arguments.

In a Female Led Relationship, a woman is set free. She is free to make decisions about her desires and those of her spouse or partners. She is no longer controlled by a man, and by allowing herself to feel her Goddess power, she furthers her evolution. The Female Led Relationship is here to stay, and women are no longer tolerating abuse, control, and bad behavior of men. Even in seemingly good relationships, a woman can be made to feel controlled and left sexually unfulfilled. The mere idea of sex for a man's orgasm and pleasure is one of the main reasons women are changing.

What works for a man does not work for a woman, and as more research is done into women's biology, physiology, and psychology the more we realize that change is not only imminent but necessary. Patriarchy is over, and the Female Led Relationship will usher in a new era, one where women will take charge and men will be the supportive gentleman. This new role for men should never be viewed as weakness as there is great responsibility in being the supporter. I have always believed that women were meant to lead. They are more suited to lead as they are armed with better communications styles, flexibility, empathy, and intuition.

Patriarchy dictated in biblical stories that in the story of Adam and Eve, Adam disobeyed God and took the apple from Eve, his wife. This is how it was taught to me. But as far back as when I was a child in Catholic schools, I felt that we can interpret this story as Adam obeyed his wife Eve and did what she wanted, even at the risk of disobeying God, classic LR.

Since the dawn of time, men have served women. Why did men go out and hunt and do the manual work? Because each day, their duty was to provide service for their women who remained home, took care of the household and the children. The strength of the home and the household is one of the most important tasks and provides a foundation on which humans can operate. Women were leaders in ensuring that everything in the home was taken care of. Only in the case of attempting to control women and suppress their power was being at home considered a weakness. The conditioning from patriarchy kept women down for decades, but now everything is changing.

In the past, the world was run by men but male authoritative relationships are not as effective. They don't work. The divorce rate is hovering around 50 percent. This is the result of dominant male relationships in the last 50 to 100 years. It is interesting to note that because of the breakdown in the household, with more households run by single moms, the world evolved to be female led.

Male leadership only leads to conflict, arguments, and growing apart. Wars are a male idea. Fighting, in general, is a male idea. Rarely do you see two women getting into a physical altercation. Women in same-sex couples are rarely reported for domestic abuse. Why? Because it is part of the male led paradigm. When women feel ignored and pressured by men, they generally start spending more time with friends who make them feel appreciated and allow open communication.

Many women feel they must suppress a feeling of superiority in fear of upsetting their man's fragile ego. This leads to women feeling underappreciated and stifled. Eventually, a woman hiding the need to feel her power becomes depressed, disgruntled, and angry. Men, you don't want to be in a relationship with an angry woman. My simple advice is to be obedient to your woman. Even if you have not always obeyed in the past, you must obey her now. Allow yourself to be directed by the commands of your woman. When a woman sees you respect her for good choices and intelligent decisions, she will change her conduct and be pleased by your behavior. Then, you will be rewarded. When you reward a woman like a Queen, she will rise to embody a Queen, which means more happiness as you will be proud to be at her side, serving her.

When women are treated like Queens, they will take on the role in their appearance, behavior, and outlook, which will inspire you to be more of a gentleman. You will worship your woman's intelligence, heart, and beauty. Your woman will take command of your heart as you submit to her, and she will guide you wisely by the imperishable beauty of her gentle and loving authority over you, which is very precious.

Simone de Beauvoir and her book *The Second Sex* is credited with spearheading the women's movement. Her writing explained why it was difficult for talented women to become successful. The obstacles de Beauvoir cites include women's inability to make as much money as men do in the same profession, women's domestic responsibilities, society's lack of support toward talented women, and women's fear that success will lead to an annoyed husband or prevent them from even finding a husband at all. She also argues that women lack ambition because of how they are raised, noting that girls are told to follow the duties of their mothers, whereas boys are told to exceed the accomplishments of their fathers.

Along with other influences, Simone de Beauvoir's work helped the feminist movement to erupt, causing the formation of le Mouvement de Libération des Femmes or the Women's Liberation Movement. Contributors to the Women's Liberation Movement include Simone de Beauvoir, Christiane Rochefort, Christine Delphy, and Anne Tristan. Through this movement, women gained equal rights such as the right to an education, a right to work, and a right to vote.

There are many other reasons why an FLR is so appealing to women. If we look at some of the attributes important to women, like finding an empathetic, understanding man who is a good listener. Women love to communicate and talk, so they desire a thoughtful listener, which men must practice and work on regularly. Men who are in Female Led Relationships or desire being in one will tend to be more in touch with their deeper emotional side, and therefore, are accustomed to women who communicate well. They tend to develop these skills, which strong, dominant women desire. Men who are good listeners are present and attentive, not just waiting until it's their turn to talk, and they are able to follow the rhythm of a good discussion and adapt to it.

Couples who don't learn to consciously communicate will face issues in intimacy, conflict, and relational growth. Understanding your Queen's inner world and having them understand yours is pivotal to true connection, and most women desire this connection in a Female Led Relationship. Lastly, plethora of evidence reveals that females are superior to men in many ways. Science proves this. Dr. Sharon Moalem, a Canadian physician and scientist, says the extra X in every female cell, far from being redundant, is instrumental in ensuring that women have a distinct genetic advantage.

Humans have 23 chromosome pairs. One of those pairs consists of our two sex chromosomes. Females have two X chromosomes (XX), males have one X, one Y (XY). The X chromosome has about 1000 genes; the Y has maybe 70. The X is one of the biggest chromosomes and contains extremely significant genes, which makes and maintains the brain.

Why did nature give females a double dose of the superior chromosome? In addition, 5,000 known species of mammals are female led. Killer whales are a great example of a species that lives long and is led by the oldest females. Mark van Vugt, an evolutionary psychology professor at VU University Amsterdam, says, "Leadership is something that happens because there is a problem that needs to be solved by some kind of coordinated action." It seems nature has determined that when problem-solving, finding food, avoiding predators, or resolving conflict, females may be better suited. Women everywhere know the future is female.

CHAPTER 3

Why Do Men Like Female Led Relationships?

W hy do men like Female Led Relationships? After helping thousands of couples, and specifically men with their marriages and finding suitable partners, I believe that men are indeed inspired by strong capable women, ultimately desiring a woman they can treat like a Queen. Men are looking for the woman who captures them, excites them, and someone they can be proud of.

Research shows that two-thirds of men fall in love with a woman very similar to their mother, so men will be attracted to women who have similar qualities to their mothers, as this is the person they tend to love and respect the most. Relationship expert Rachel Lloyd says, "It's well known that we tend to migrate toward people who share similar traits with us and, to varying degrees, we seek to recreate aspects of our original relationships with our parents." Research shows that our earliest relationships, especially with our mother, influence how we can connect as adults in romantic and other contexts and also create internalized scripts or working models of how relationships work.

Other factors may be driving the need for a strong woman. Today men are under a tremendous amount of stress and anxiety about relationships, love, and life, and it's even more difficult having to find their place in a world where women are dominating. They must resolve their issues with patriarchal conditioning from childhood and how they think they're supposed to be as a modern man existing in this new world.

Since men are still expected to take on leadership positions in their working life, they are happy to take less of this role in their personal life. Therefore, Female Led Relationships takes the stress of a leadership role off of men who would prefer not to have the pressure. It releases them from a role of authority that they might otherwise have been pressured to take at home and at work. Some men would prefer to adopt the gentler role in a relationship, such as looking after children, tending to the home, cooking and cleaning, and earning less income without the stress of being the breadwinner.

Men in Female Led Relationships can appreciate their partner more and better recognize their worth. They see their partners as equals, rather than as below them. A Female Led Relationship also helps a man learn to serve and worship his woman better as he gains more of an understanding about what really turns women on and how to communicate better. They have the opportunity to evolve in an FLR with the help of their Queen.

Men are attracted to a strong, confident woman because today they want to be proud to serve a Queen, not a maid, and they are addicted to the chase. A strong woman represents the trophy. Sure, he likes to be mothered and taken care of from time to time, but men need unpredictability and excitement. That's where a strong woman comes in, and in a Female Led Relationship, men desire to serve.

Let's face it, confident women are winners in the board and the bedroom, so confidence is sexy and a real turn-on. Strong women know how to please their men in bed and demand what they want, and this is just too irresistible to pass up. Think Sharon Stone in the movie *Basic Instinct* or Mila Jovovich in the movie *Resident Evil*. What man can resist a real temptress?

The alpha woman is looking for an absolutely independent man, both financially and psychologically. He must have a healthy ego and his own opinion, hobbies, and friends. An alpha woman is looking for an equal partner, someone to walk with, not behind or in front of.

One thing that men will appreciate in a strong woman is her deep appreciation for her freedom, and she truly appreciates a man who respects that. Women can't stand being restricted in any way. Men love their freedom too, so this can be a win-win situation once you ensure there is adequate time spent together and intimately. Strong women want to be challenged. They want to compete with their partner intellectually, physically, and emotionally. Men will be often kept on their toes at all times, and it's almost impossible to ignore or dismiss a powerful woman who also likes to push herself, is ambitious, successful, and capable. These are all qualities admired in other men, so they are often thrilled when they find these very qualities in a woman they are attracted to.

Today couples are searching for ways to keep their relationship and interaction intense, intimate, and exciting. Female Led Relationships and female led marriages offer more ways to keep life interesting with several additional areas to explore. Maybe your Queen desires cuckolding, or maybe you both want to add the element of domination and submission with spanking, BDSM, and role-playing. Maybe you prefer the freedom of consensual non-monogamy where you can be in a committed relationship and have the freedom to explore additional partners.

The ways to switch things up are endless, and men love the variety as well. Men crave a woman who is naturally mysterious and exciting. That's what keeps the spice alive. Too often, couples get into a rut that they cannot get out of because the source of regular relationships is the outdated paradigm of patriarchy. Most women, if they are honest, do not want to be a slave to a man. She's not going to choose, giving her man a blow job or having intercourse for 5 to 10 minutes then having everything done once he cums over her own pleasure and desires. Too often women who are stuck in regular relationships are unhappy at the core because they remain unsatisfied. Men can sense when the Queen is angry and unfulfilled and places even more strain on the relationship.

In an FLR, both you and the Queen are focused on each other's needs every day. The tendency to grow apart and become bored is rare because the focus is inward. You place her on a pedestal and learn to worship her properly, and she, in turn, rewards you with more excitement, good regular sex, and a general sense of positivity and happiness. Men desire a purring kitty over a vicious lioness any day.

CHAPTER 4

Types of Female Led Relationships

A ll relationships and marriages are not equal and even Female Led Relationships can take on different forms. Everything from the levels of control to whether there will be other daily rules and customs (like discipline) to whether there will be consensual non-monogamy in terms of hotwifing and cuckolding. No matter what happens, the foundation of a Female Led Relationship is that the woman is in charge.

Here are the different levels of control in a Female Led Relationship:

Level One

The lowest level of an FLR woman involves having a limited amount of control and taking the lead on some decisions, but not all. Her dominance could also spill over into the bedroom, which can make for a more exciting sex life. In general, at the lowest level, couples will be starting out on their FLR journey. Typically, the man will show his service to the Queen by allowing her to take control of daily activities, outings, kid's schedules, and TV viewing. This is a great way to begin your female led journey and helps your Queen to become accustomed to taking the lead. Consider this to be the springboard for moving on to other levels.

This is also a good time for men to learn how to adapt to their role as supportive gentlemen. You both can work out the complexities of adopting these new roles, and it can represent the turning point for going from a normal relationship to FLR. Though this light level is rarely depicted, it is an important entry point for most couples who want to build a successful long-term relationship.

Level Two

In the next level of a Female Led Relationship, the woman's role as the dominant partner begins to get a little more serious. She will start to call the shots on more areas of the relationship and dominate her man in the bedroom more too. The man may take on more traditionally "female" roles in the relationship, such as taking care of the household, handling the kids, and completing more chores.

At this level, your Queen will take responsibility for the daily schedules and maybe have a written agenda of duties. She will generally control the finances and decide on activities, the delegation of household duties, and any other serious decisions to be made. She may also decide on how sex should progress and if as a couple you will begin to explore cuckolding, hotwifing or any other ways to spice up the sex life.

This second level is great for couples who are happy with the beginning level and have done so for at least six months. Do not proceed to this level if there was major hesitation at the lowest level. At this point, you should be happy and excited to already be in a Female Led Relationship. Many couples remain at this point and are perfectly happier staying here.

Level Three

The third level of an FLR involves complete submission to the Queen's desires. It's her way or the highway. Men must learn to submit completely, and I recommend that you start your study with my book *Turning Point*, which will help you to address any past conditioning that might be holding you back. It is at this level that the Queen may introduce hotwifing, cuckolding, spanking, and some BDSM if she desires. She may want to direct all of your sexual activities.

Your duty to her to serve her each and every day will become extremely important. She may decide that chastity and orgasm control is necessary, and she may prohibit masturbation to ensure all of your focus is on her. You will treat her like a Queen at all times, never interrupt her, never raise your voice to her, and spend every moment ensuring that she is pleased. She will also have the responsibility of assuming complete control and directing all activities, events, and happenings in the household. She may take over the finances.

Sex is for the Queen's pleasure, and you must ensure that your oral skills are perfected. You can refer to my book *Oral Sex for Women*, which you will get all the necessary instruction needed to properly pleasure your Queen. You must satisfy her needs before your own. Communication will be mandatory at this point because you will need to identify what her needs are and what changes must be made. You need to be communicating every step of the way.

Level Four

The most extreme level of a Female Led Relationship is where the Queen demands that her man be her servant. Most couples don't need to get to this level, but many love the extremes of it. The man can be sissified, and he can literally become the servant to his Queen. She may decide to place him in a cage or in a time-out corner, punish him, do spanking, bondage, and more. She may decide on cuckolding and having her Bull over while her man serves you both. There often is a formal contract created to outline the duties of her man to service the Queen.

Even though this level is extreme, there must still be full consent from both you and your Queen. You must analyze if you truly derive pleasure from being in servitude, locked up, and completely controlled sometimes in an inhumane way. Your Queen also must decide if this is what she wants. This extreme level is reserved for those couples who are fully on board with taking their FLR to an extreme level. The activities at this level are not mandatory. A reverse example of this was in the movie *Fifty Shades of Grey*. Christian required Anna to sign a contract and be at his beck and call at all times. She also had to experience spankings and many sessions in his private room.

Similarly, in the reverse, this is what happens in a Female Led Relationship at the extreme level. Safe words must be implemented and communication about boundaries become very important and must not be skipped. Some couples enjoy the formality of the Queen dressed in leather and latex, and you, the man dressed as a sissy or submissive clothing of her choice. She may decide what clothes you wear, where you go out, and she may decide she wants you to be collared and pegged on a regular basis. The important thing to remember is that you both want to take your relationship to this level and there is a mutual agreement.

It is important to understand the difference between being a dominatrix and a Queen. The *Love & Obey* version of the Female Led Relationship lies between level one and level three. Though I am aware that level four happens, a Female Led Relationship has to function as a successful relationship or marriage first, and this can be accomplished with loving Female Led Relationship without the cages, whips, contracts, and sissification.

The media loves to portray dominant women as cruel and inhumane, but this is neither conducive to building a successful marriage or interaction nor will it necessarily lead to long-term success. I always think back to the General Adaptation Syndrome (GAS) by Hans Selye, in which he says that an organism under stress can become stronger if the stressor is only intermittent. If the stressor is continual and prolonged, the organism eventually dies. I believe that the same is true for relationships—cruelty can only go so far before it becomes destructive. The aim of a woman taking control is not to be cruel, though it happens with dominatrixes and their clients. The difference is that a dominatrix gets paid to administer what the man wants in terms of cruelty, punishment, and discipline as part of his deep-seated desires. Because essentially, she is being paid to do what a man desires, which is not female led in my view.

So, it is not advisable for your Queen to become a dominatrix in order to be female led. If she wishes to insert some dominance and fun practices like light spanking, BDSM, dressing up in leather to spice up your fun, sexy times, then this is permissible. A Female Led Relationship is only successful if it is loving and both people can feel appreciated, loved, and respected in their roles. Your Queen will still be loving and sexual while she leads, and you can still be respectful and supportive while being submissive.

There are many reasons why men and women choose a Female Led Relationship. In some instances, it's a simple case of an aggressive woman and a passive man falling into place naturally. In other cases, an alpha man recognizes the benefits that her leadership would bring to the relationship, and convinces, teaches or reprograms her man to accept her loving female authority over him and gives him proper direction. These teachings have led me to understand the rules that men must observe to create the best Female Led Relationship.

If men understand these rules early on, women will experience less stress and anxiety with having to train or reprogram their men on how to behave and serve daily. If men follow the rules, the relationship will be generally positive, rewarding, and fulfilling for both genders. When your Queen is at peace and more relaxed, she is able to give more love and affection to her man, making him happier than he ever thought possible. This type of relationship is a win-win because both of you are the happiest you have ever been. Men desire and women want to be desired. It's perfect harmony.

CHAPTER 5

Benefits of a Female Led Household

There are numerous advantages for a relationship where the female is leading the household. This type of relationship ensures that the household benefits from streamlined decision-making by the woman. Consensus and acceptance are never good approaches to decision-making as it leads to compromise. Compromise means that neither party is 100 percent happy, and any decision is less than optimal. Empowering the wife or girlfriend to make all the decisions brings order, stability, and predictability to a relationship. More than anything, it ensures a lack of dispute and argument, which results in a harmonious union.

In addition, men have found that when they assume the role of serving their women, they feel empowered because their women feel much happier and supported for being able to get what they want. The Female Led Relationship is a win-win situation for both. The outcome is fewer headaches, arguments, and disagreements, giving more time to having fun and feeling connected with open communication.

I discovered that couples in a Female Led Relationship experience more harmony because each person is clear on their roles and code of conduct. Your Queen will make sure that what needs to be done in your home is done at the right time, completed in the right order, and is performed well. In any wife led marriage, she decides what is important for her man to do at any given time. If the man is in agreement, then the relationship is smooth.

However, the challenge occurs when women and men are unsure of their roles, and this struggle exists when couples want "equality" in a relationship. I often have this conversation with my friends who are leaders and professionals in their careers. How often does anything get accomplished if everyone in the firm is equal and there is no leader? They usually never agree. It's the same with relationships. Women have been led to believe that the best we can hope for is equality, but equality leads to disagreement.

At some point, someone needs to take leadership in making the decisions and managing the day-to-day activities in the relationship. There can be understandings and "suggestions" by both partners but, in general, leadership is necessary in work at home. The woman must have the final say. Men submit to their women as a knight would to his Queen.

Generally, women are more adept at leading at home, and they make most of the decisions, even in traditional marriages. So, for men, this is often easily accepted as the way it should be. In FLR, it is enhanced because the woman knows they have a supportive, obedient partner. This obedience only makes the woman happier and more loving to her man.

This year, I released my book *Mommy's in Charge* to help parents with teaching their kids about female led and female empowerment. When a mom is leading, she is inspiring the younger generation and the entire household is prepared for the challenges of living in a society which will eventually be run by women. It's more than likely that your children will be managed by female bosses and will experience female leadership in the future. Research by Refinery29 showed that 40 percent of households are run by women and 37 percent make more than their husbands.

Thirty years ago, in married, heterosexual households, a male partner was generally the primary breadwinner and considered the head of household. Even among married two-earner households, it is increasingly common to see women as the head. Among married households, the share of women heads of household increased 24.3 percentage points, from 21.8 percent in 1990 to 46.1 percent in 2019. Even among married two-earner households, it is increasingly common to see women as the head. Among married households, the share of women heads of household increased 24.3 percentage points, from 21.8 percent in 1990 to 46.1 percent in 2019.

To demonstrate the growth of female led, in 1990, only 32.5 percent of households were headed by women. Over the next three decades, the share of households headed by women increased 17 percentage points, and by 2019, households headed by women accounted for half of all households. Education has a big part to play where over the past 30 years, the share of women who are heads of household and have a bachelor's degree increased from 17 percent to 35 percent. Despite the shrinking education gap, women still earn less than men. The median income of households headed by women is almost $20,000 lower than those headed by men. There is no question that females are taking charge of households and are becoming more influential in the modern family and the workforce, which changes the dynamic of relationships and marriages.

CHAPTER 6

How to Reignite the Passion with a Female Led Relationship

Your marriage or relationship is one of the most important aspects in life. It's one where you share everything with your Queen. When you get together, you have a strong desire to be with that person. You often think about her night and day and want to spend every waking moment with her. The passion is both mental and physical; they encompass your every thought and you yearn to be with her. That unbridled, untouched deep feeling can sometimes start to fade. Why does it happen and how can we reignite the passion?

Real life gets in the way, and other priorities take precedence. When we are dating, she is the focus, but as time goes on and children, friends, family, hobbies, and work are added into the mix, these parts of our lives can start to take our attention away from the Queen. Soon we are ignoring her desires and wishes in favor of our own, and pretty soon, this escalates into forming distance between you.

Less Effort

In the beginning, things are fresh and new. You want to look your best and try to impress her. But as time goes on, you don't feel the same pressure or desire to try your hardest. We slip into disrespectful behavior, and we behave badly. It turns into habits that eventually become common. Everything becomes routine and comfortable. The excitement fades. Boredom and monotony are the kiss of death in a relationship, and it takes real work to try to change up our routines. We adhere to the same schedules, eat the meals, watch the same show, and have sex in the same positions.

Pretty soon, this boredom has you thinking of ways to change it up with outside interests or people. The reason cheating doesn't solve anything for long is that while you change the person up, you do not change, and after a while, you get settled into a routine with your outside activities as much as your main relationship. Soon the cheating gets boring too, or worse, you get caught, and it destroys your entire marriage and life.

You get comfortable in your appearance and soon you are unattractive to your Queen, and maybe you are less interested in her. Being unattractive to your partner is the beginning of the downward spiral because once the sexual attraction is gone, then the interest wanes, and you are essentially friends or roommates.

Stress and Responsibilities

Let's face it, life is filled with complications, challenges, and stress. It may be bad enough that you barely have the energy to go to work and handle all the responsibilities of life, but now having to change up your marriage or relationship is another complication. Intimacy and connection fade as you spend less time together. Because life takes you in so many directions and a busy schedule can leave less time to do things together with your Queen, you begin to spend less and less time together, and this is where the distancing begins.

But all of this can be turned around, one step at a time. First, you need to get in touch with how you felt when you first met. Things were spontaneous, fun, and exciting. You were exploring each other. This is what you have to do with your Queen. Decide to force yourselves to try something new. Some couples go out and hire a sex therapist, who will counsel you on certain things you can do to improve the intensity during sex. But long before this, you can make mini changes that can make all the difference.

First, focus on yourself. Have you let yourself go? When was the last time you were in the gym? If it's been a while, it may be time to revisit. When was the last time you went shopping for new gear? Or got a hip new haircut? Shave your beard or grow a beard? Maybe you liked rock climbing, surfing, or hiking—these are activities you need to get back to. Maybe do it with your Queen. Join a bowling league or a new church. Make some new friends. The idea is to inject newness in some form into both of your lives. Once this begins to feel inspiring, it leads to other changes. Set aside one day of the week for date night—you both go out, have a cocktail, flirt, and have some conversation with others.

Many couples take a short getaway to a sexy resort or a weekend in the Hamptons. The more you can get out of your rut of day-to-day life, the more you will begin to feel the way you did when you were dating. As a man, you only need to start doing romantic things. Make her feel special. If there's a sure shot way to get your Queen's love and attention, it is to make them feel special. Bake a cake for her, buy his favorite drink, or give them a massage. Bring her flowers. Yes, she may grumble that you spent the money, but secretly she's impressed. Get her favorite dessert.

I can recall being at a low point in my relationship, and my partner surprised me with one night away, where he had strewn my favorite chocolate bars across the room, and the centerpiece was my favorite dessert. We spent the whole night watching all of my favorite movies and having bubble baths. It was short, but it made all the difference. It reaffirmed to me that he cared and wanted to try. If you don't try you don't succeed. Turning around a relationship can be one of the most challenging things, but it can be done.

Most couples begin a Female Led Relationship as the turnaround because the minute men begin to commit to worship their Queen, it changes everything. Have conversations laying out what your new life can look like. You have been together for a reason. Many men think that the answer lies in finding someone new, but this is not necessarily the solution, as you have not changed integral parts of your personality, so you are likely to attract exactly what you think you need to get rid of. Real change begins inside. Once you begin to change and your Queen is onboard to make changes as well, the relationship undergoes transformation. A lot of what most people want can be found with your partner or spouse that you are comfortable with. You just need to take initiative to make the changes.

Another great way to change things is to start touching her again. Physical touch, whether it's kissing, handholding, hugging, or cuddling, will steam up your relationship. So, include touch in your everyday routine. Smack her butt, kiss her for no reason, touch her hand, hold hands. Explore her body and touch areas you never had before. Your familiarity after being together for some time helps you to feel comfortable trying new positions, techniques, or locations.

Sex is an essential ingredient to spice up your relationship. Don't let any excuses come in your way when it comes to having sex. If your Queen is too tired, arouse them through a sensuous massage with essential oils or light up the bedroom with aromatic candles. When was the last time you ate whip cream off of her. Combine dessert with sexy sexual exploration.

There are four types of chemistry which will help you and your Queen get the spark back in your life:

1. **Physical chemistry:** it generates physical desire and arousal

2. **Emotional chemistry:** this creates care, affection, and trust

3. **Mental chemistry:** generates interest, compatibility, and receptivity

4. **Spiritual chemistry:** brings respect, appreciation, happiness

When people complain about being bored in their relationship, they often cite being stuck in a rut or routine. Then there is the worry about how to keep the relationship alive. They may feel a sudden desire for novelty and assume that novelty can only come from a new partner or moving homes. One of the biggest issues is the tendency for the primary relationship to begin to break down. Here is a summary of everything you can do to keep the spice alive in your Female Led Relationship:

Reinforce Your Relationship Daily

Remind her of the love you both feel daily. Kiss, hug, greet her as the Queen, and don't allow the relationship to take a backseat. In our busy world, we tend to place other matters above the relationship, and only when going out do we make a big deal. We make excuses for being busy, tired, or just not in the mood. Now more than ever, you both will need to spend time on the relationship.

Take Care of Your Health and Fitness

Often so much is going on that we barely have time to worry about the upkeep of our health and fitness. Only when you are healthy and feel good about yourself, can you take care of your partner. So, remember to eat right, stay fit, and sleep well. A healthy body results in a healthy mind and that clearly reflects in your relationship. Remain attractive to both of you. This increases the sexiness of all the other activities.

Spend Time Together

It is important to spend quality time together with just the two of you. Going out with the kids is not considered quality time together. You still need a date night and maybe picnics in the park, bike rides, or just hanging out. I can recall a couple who was married for 27 years and introduced all sorts of extras into the relationship, and they had lunch together every single day to simply talk. It worked. Their relationship was able to withstand any obstacle.

Give Her Space

Being in a relationship doesn't mean that you have to be together every second of the day. She still needs to meet with her friends, and you still need the beer night with the boys. Allow each other to have time to spend alone as well.

Help with Chores

There is a reason why 80 percent of women complain about being too tired to have sex or do anything. Women have to excel in their careers and take care of the kids, the household, and your needs. It's an exhausting life. Any help you give to your Queen will help her and keep her in a sexier mood.

Make Her Feel Special

Every day is an opportunity to make your Queen feel special. You have so many chances to compliment her, leave her love notes, bring her flowers and make her feel like she is the luckiest person in the world. Not only will she be in a better mood, but she will also respond in a positive way, and it keeps the focus on you and not the cuckolding as much. The truth is, every interaction we have with another person, even someone we've known for a long time, is a new possibility for lively connection. It often takes only a small action—a sweet smile, a flirtatious look, or an act of affection to turn a mundane interaction into an exciting one. These are simple ways to make your Queen feel special. Check her out and give her that sexy look like she is the most gorgeous woman on the planet.

Keep Touching

Touch is so important in relationships. Whether it's kissing, handholding, hugging, or cuddling—all keep the spice alive. Touch her hair, her back, and her legs often. Squeeze her butt as you go by. Kiss for no reason and hold hands. Touch keeps the focus on you both.

Set the Scene

Just as you would prepare for your big night out, you also need to keep the primary space sexy. Draw her a bath, lay out some lingerie, get her favorite bubbles, get some wine or champagne, and massage oils. You want to show dedication and effort. Men always complain that they don't understand why women are upset. Women desire the fantasy of an open relationship without having to explain every step. You want to show this woman that even though you engage in open relationships, the primary relationship with her is what you need. Make a special dinner with candlelight for her. There is no need to wait for a special moment to make her feel special and loved.

Have Sex Regularly

Your sex life still needs to be great and regular. One of the first major indicators that a relationship is breaking down is the frequency of sex. So, it is very important that you have a great sex life and you keep it alive. It is recommended that your own sex be where you connect deeply as a couple. Add some oral sex or long foreplay to really connect with your Queen. Remember getting her into the mood begins early on in the day, from the moment she wakes up you want to put her in the mood.

Be Truthful

Studies have found that people who are truthful about themselves experience more relationship intimacy and well-being. They also have better romantic relationships. Overall, studies find that positive connection and intimacy grow when you are transparent about what's inside of you. A recent study by the University of Georgia looked at the connection between communication and the degree of satisfaction reported by couples. It found that good communication in itself could not account for how satisfied partners were with a relationship over time.

The researchers recognize that other factors must influence couples' satisfaction and that good communication can result from those factors. According to Justin Lavner, lead author of the study, found that more satisfied couples communicate better on average than those who are less satisfied. So, what will make you and your Queen more satisfied is the happiness you feel together and being truthful and honest about your feelings throughout your exploration.

CHAPTER 7

Female Led Relationship Sex

What is Female Led Relationship sex like? FLR sex can be the most exciting, exhilarating, and fun you've ever experienced. The reason FLR sex is so exciting to couples is because it helps unleash and free the Queen. Once women can explore their sexuality and taking control in bed, they tend to enjoy sex more, and it offers infinite ways to explore all sorts of sex positions, toys, role-play, BDSM, and open relationships.

In a Female Led Relationship, the Queen isn't waiting for you to satisfy her. You must find ways to ensure that you focus on her pleasure, and if you cannot perform, she is entitled to explore other opportunities. Part of keeping your Queen completely satisfied, happy, and in a great mood every single day, is satisfying her with great oral sex. Boring sex creates boring relationships, which don't last long. Most women report being unsatisfied.

Studies show that 25 percent to 74 percent of women have faked an orgasm, so chances are your Queen has as well. But think of how life would be if you gave your Queen a mind-blowing orgasm every day. Female led sex is all about how to fully satisfy your woman by placing her pleasure first. You will be making it your mission, if you choose to accept it, to make her orgasm the focus of your sex. You will become a pro at giving her the best oral sex she has ever had, which will keep her coming back for more.

Not only is this going to change the dynamics of your relationship, but you are going to reap the rewards of a happy wife, happy life. Oral sex is also crucial to your Queen's well-being and her health. You might be surprised by how much you enjoy it, not to mention the attention you get in return. You may have tried all the sex positions and role-play, but at the end of the day, you are giving your Goddess the gift that she (and her vibrator) can't give her: mind-blowing oral sex.

A significant part of finding and keeping a female led woman is that a man must show his complete service to her. Part of this service is being a great lover. Why has Casanova been remembered for centuries? Not because he was great at his job or he could fix cars. If you're going to keep your woman happy, you will need to master the bedroom, which means becoming a pro at fully satisfying your woman with oral sex.

Oral sex has been around for centuries and is called by several names: cunnilingus, and slang terms like going down, going downtown, eating her out, pussy licking, sucking clam or sucking oysters, munching carpet, or perhaps some other equally ridiculous slang term commonly used to describe it. Although there are a variety of slang terms people use to describe giving oral sex pleasure to a woman, we are going to call it with the proper respect it deserves, female led oral sex.

Oral sex, to a woman, is the most important skill you will need to master if you want to call yourself a great lover. Your woman will probably orgasm more from oral sex than when having intercourse alone, and this is a win-win situation for both of you. Part of oral sex is understanding how it relates to Goddess worship and reaching the divine.

It is generally accepted that when a penis is erect or when a vagina is wet, it means a person is primed and ready for sex. This isn't always the case, yet our cultural discourse around sex and arousal has led us to incorrectly assume that a person's physical response to sexual stimulation is aligned with their level of desire.

In reality, there are many times when desire and physical arousal don't match. In fact, physical arousal is different from subjective arousal which is the active mental engagement in sex. It is this confusion that can lead to you or your Queen remaining unfulfilled and sex becoming lackluster. It is the mental engagement and deep connection along with physical intimacy that makes female led sex so exciting and desirable.

The Female Led Relationship offers the freedom to explore with consent from both of you and with lots of communication. Even though the woman makes the rules in a Female Led Relationship, everything still requires an agreement from both of you. Women have admitted that some of the benefits are having your needs taken care of, deciding who does which chore, handling the money, and not having to ask permission for any purchase, having a greater sense of power and control than your outside life might have, and being more dominant in your sex life. Many couples in normal relationships are exploring a female led lifestyle because many men have the fantasy of serving a strong woman and being dominated by one.

In my experience, it is mostly men who first discover and want to initiate the change to female led, but once his Queen is involved, the relationship begins to evolve quickly. Men tend to take charge during work and deal with the stress of having major responsibilities. Many are happy for their woman to take the lead at home, and they simply submit to her leadership. They look forward to when their woman comes home and tells them it's time to cook dinner, rub her feet, clean the house, or give her pleasure. It's liberating to relinquish control and give in to her every desire.

One way your Queen can be sexy while showing her dominance and leadership is saying, "If you finish all your chores tonight, I might let you go down on me later." This is a great practice because it gives you a goal and gets you both into a sexy state of mind. Each day is a new opportunity to explore how you will serve your Queen sexually and how she can entice you to be the best lover you can be. My book *Oral Sex for Women* is the perfect in-depth guide to being an oral pro. In a Female Led Relationship, there is no "wham bam, thank you, ma'am." Sex is for your Queen's pleasure and whether she is sexually satisfied is your responsibility.

If your Queen has to resort to faking orgasms or pretending to enjoy sex when she'd rather be doing anything else, this is a failure on your part and must be changed. Oral sex done properly will change your sex life, and more importantly, your woman's sex life. Ultimately, it can make you and your woman have a great love life together, and sharing love between people is what it is all about in life. Oral sex should never be faked, played, or simulated. If you don't want to give her oral sex, it's the same as her not wanting to have intercourse with you.

You may orgasm easily during sex, but most women don't. In addition, if she's not enjoying oral sex because your technique is off or you don't know what you are doing, this can be the beginning of a disaster. Unhappy wife, disastrous life. Today, it is important for men to learn how to master oral sex if they're going to keep a strong, demanding Queen in a Female Led Relationship happy. Bad oral sex makes a woman feel uncomfortable and makes you seem unsure of yourself. Don't do as the comedian Sam Kinison instructs. He said, "You perform oral sex on a woman by writing out the letters of the alphabet with your tongue on a woman's clitoris." This gets you in the doghouse really fast and leaves you with a raging, unhappy, unsatisfied woman.

Learning how to give proper oral sex will teach you how to truly serve your Goddess and make love to her with your mouth and tongue. I will show you how to achieve a mind-blowing orgasm, which I call the *cosmic orgasm*. It is so powerful that you will feel like you're having an orgasm with her as she comes into your mouth. The Divine Oral Sex I am describing can result in true joy and spiritual orgasm that will heal your soul and make you feel like the king of the world. It will be the greatest enhancement of your love life within your present relationship and will unlock a new level of passion between you and your woman.

To become an artist and deliver divine bliss to your woman, you must be genuinely devoted to loving, obeying, and serving her and putting her pleasure first. The power of love will give you the strength, purity of heart, and connection to the feminine divine to dissolve anything and all that might still be separating you at this very moment from achieving the ultimate cosmic orgasm with your Goddess.

So, take a look inside, gentleman, observe your very own present attitude and feelings toward your present female partner, and make proper adjustments and give total freedom to your partner. Do you want to commit and make your partner fully happy right now? Do you want to make a genuine effort to achieve love, be obedient to her, and serve all her needs and bring her pleasure, or not? Do you want your partner to find true love and absolute long-lasting bliss and happiness in your relationship? If you want to unleash the real sexual beast of your Queen, then, this is how you do it.

The Female Led Relationship offers an opportunity to explore more than just a great daily life with your queen. It gives you a chance to improve all aspects of her life, making her a greater leader and a more confident woman and connecting to her on the deepest level possible. Oral sex is the pathway to the divine. The vagina and uterus give life, and many believe it is a connection to the spiritual realm. Why is this important? Humans are not just physical creatures. We are mental, physical, and spiritual beings, and many times unhappiness in individuals and relationships can stem from the inability to satisfy all parts.

As the man in your Queen's life, you learned it was your duty to ensure your woman feels fully served. In daily life, this is accomplished by doing everything she commands and allowing her to take control in all aspects of your life. Sex is an extremely important part of your service, and now you will be able to connect to her on levels that no one else can. In the bedroom, you will now be charged with giving your Queen the ultimate sexual experience by making the sex all about her and placing the focus on her.

By doing this, you will gain great pleasure as well. You will not only feel more satisfied in your own orgasms, but you will be confident that you are solely responsible for giving her the ultimate sexual pleasure. Oral sex becomes the center of the entire sexual session because the act is the main method most women require to climax effectively. Now you become the most important person in her life. One of the exciting parts of a FLR is sharing as many new experiences in your daily life as possible.

Now, as a man, you are supporting your woman on her path to connecting to the Feminine Divine, the Divine Cosmic

Force of the Universe. This divine connection will enhance your present relationship and bring new energy into your life. Tantric masters have long preached the importance of sexual energy. This is so powerful that they use it to transcend. They learn techniques to expand and deepen the orgasm experience. In female led oral sex, this is what you are doing for your Goddess.

Sex becomes the ritual you will perform throughout the entire session to help your Goddess have that mind-blowing cosmic experience together with her orgasm. Your sex becomes a ceremony, a celebration of the divine. You become more connected to the universe when you bring your Goddess to orgasm, and you are also experiencing euphoria. In tantric sex, the male energy is like fire—burning hot and fast, but a woman's energy is like water—it flows. It is this difference that makes female led oral sex so much more complex. You will no longer think of your male ego or your male pleasure. You will no longer receive oral sex or a blow job unless your Goddess desires it for her own reasons. You will now live to bring pleasure to your Goddess first. Once her needs are fulfilled, then you can fulfill yours.

The difference with focusing on her pleasure is that it takes a very precise technique to be able to get her sufficiently aroused and to ensure she is satisfied. The entire sex session is done with her at the center. I raise the example of Henry VIII. Only Anne Boleyn, who made Henry wait to have sex until they were married and controlled his every mood, received his undivided attention during sex. Henry had thousands of lovers who he just fucked and left, but Anne forced him to learn to seduce her and place her above even his closest advisors. This was a revolution at the time since the opinion of a woman, even at royal levels, was never considered. Women were virtually invisible. But Anne Boleyn was one of the first women at that time to essentially create a

Female Led Relationship with someone who was, at the time, the most powerful man on the planet.

That is the power of female led. Once you fully commit to satisfying your Goddess, you will receive a tremendous energy boost and strengthening of your worship of your Queen. I recommend performing oral sex on your woman as often as she will allow.

Traditional relationships approach oral sex as an added act, a naughty experiment in which both participants embark on a pleasure-seeking investigation. In a Female Led Relationship, it is the opposite. It is the main event, an opportunity to raise the vibration and connect to the spiritual realm. Cunnilingus can be perceived as naughty by patriarchal society, and these old-fashioned male-led couples may experiment to feel wicked about going down on a woman for a few minutes.

We see this portrayed in movies. I always find the movie *Fifty Shades of Grey* interesting. The film is promoted to be about BDSM in which the man is in control, but if you watch the finer aspects of the movie, you will see that the man is actually being controlled. Christian is giving Anna a lot of oral sex pleasure. Anna has the power in both her main relationship and the effects on driving other men crazy. There is only one scene where Christian Grey whips her, and after that, she puts a stop to it, essentially changing the relationship to be female led.

I believe that it is those finer points where Christian Grey is satisfying Anna completely, and there is much less focus on his own pleasure, though he tries to suggest that his perversion stems from the relationship with his mother. But in true FLR, the women are the power characters in that movie, which means it was much more about Female Led Relationships. So even the media recognizes that the old is out. Male-dominated, patriarchal, male led relationships are on the decline with female led on the rise, which makes it even more important for you to become a master of oral sex. Female leaders demand it, and you will need to give it.

Personally, I demand daily oral worship and praise of me as the Goddess. I see it as very crucial to my overall well-being. Oral sex changes a woman's eagerness for sex because she knows it's for her pleasure. How can you resist someone who wants to worship you? One of the greatest ways to show your devotion is to serve your woman's every desire, and this includes every sexual desire. It is important that you make her feel truly adored and worshipped during sex. You must allow her the time to relax and forget about all of the stresses of life. This is her moment of fantasy and adventure. Take her to another place with sex that fulfills her to the core.

Connecting to your Goddess's divine through the vagina helps to strengthen the relationship among many other health benefits. First, when you make sex about lovemaking and worship, orgasms are much easier to achieve and raise oxytocin, which helps to combat stress and regulate cortisol in the body. People sleep better, regulate appetite and hormones, and report feeling happy and positive. So, when you focus on your Goddess's pleasure, you are improving all facets of her being. You are ensuring that all aspects of her life are fulfilled. Connecting to the divine through sex improves your spiritual connection and is the most powerful way to be connected.

CHAPTER 8

How to Prepare for Mindblowing Sex

P reparation is the key to a mind-blowing sex session. In a Female Led Relationship sex becomes a ceremony, an opportunity to worship your Queen like a divine Goddess. Sex can become mundane and boring when you schedule around it and make it as a "wham bam, thank you, ma'am" event. When Sex is viewed as an opportunity for couples to fantasize, explore, push the limits and improve love-making skills, sex becomes so much more exciting.

One of the significant moments missing in sex lives is the idea of a ceremony. Lingerie, candles, and satin sheets are all part of the ceremony. I once had a conversation with a friend on Valentine's Day Eve, and I asked her what she was preparing and wearing for her husband for Valentine's night. I asked, "What kind of lingerie will you wear?" She replied, "None." She had never owned lingerie and had been married for over twenty years. I was shocked and promptly suggested she get something super sexy for the night. During FLR sex preparation and the ceremony of sex are very important, and it's the little things that add up to a fantastic experience.

So as the Queen's servant and the man, you will need to prepare for the ceremony of oral sex. Get a nice big pillow you reserve only for sex, get a fun wedge to put her hips up on, candles, massage oils— anything you can to make the space special. Buy her sexy underwear that you'll want to feel before you begin and see her walking around in. You need to partake in making sex a special experience. Reading this book is a great start because you will be able to delight her when you can show off your oral skills.

Don't feel bad if you have all these questions in your head: "Does my woman's vagina look like a mystery down there?" "What the heck do I do?" "Where do I begin?" "What's the best area to focus on?" It can be confusing. There are inner and outer flaps and folds of skin and maybe some hair, then even more folds and more flaps, and then the flower, the bud of the clitoris. "Do I lick, kiss; give rough, soft, teasing?" You will have a million questions, and I will do my best to answer them all. But remember this one guiding principle—it all works, and you need to gauge how your Queen is turned on by it. You must become very tuned into how she is feeling.

I am amazed at how many couples never discuss sex. After a sex session, it is mandatory to ask what worked, what she liked and did not like. During sex, it is fun to ask, "You like that?" "How does that feel?" These are the conversations to have, not just random, "Ooh, babe, I like that," or "Hit it hard." The worst is when men feel the need to talk all the way through. There is a time and place. Oral sex is when your woman wants to be relaxed, and you are modifying your technique to learn what works for her. It's not a session you are trying to get through so you can get to intercourse. You will approach oral sex like it's the main course, not the appetizer. We savor the main course in a meal like it's the best food we have ever had, and this is the approach you take when performing oral sex.

How to Set Up the Sexy Mood

One of the most important things to do with sex is to get your Goddess in the mood. Too many men underestimate the importance of this. If your Queen is stressed from the day, the first thing you want to do is get her to relax. This is the lead-up. Take over the chores—cooking dinner, doing the dishes, or other chores. Surprise her by drawing her a nice bath or giving her a massage. Let her unwind by discussing anything she wants to talk about. When she is relaxed, she is more likely to entertain having sex. I think surprises are a great way to show a woman you really care, and you are really interested in fulfilling her needs.

In my past regular relationships, I cannot recall one time when my partners, even in long-term relationships, brought me flowers or some other gift for no reason. I also cannot recall a time my bath was drawn or anything was done just because. Today, this happens almost every day, without me ever having to mention it. So, when you are trying to seduce your Goddess, do the unexpected. Being excited about oral sex should delight her.

Sex therapist Megan Fleming says that "all arousal begins with relaxation." How you achieve this for your woman is important. Are you supporting her in chores and household duties? Have you placed her on a pedestal calling her your Queen or Goddess? Are you light, positive, and enthusiastic? Women are going to be much more in the mood if they don't have to come home to more stressors. It's important to begin to put your woman in the mood early in the day. Send her a text saying how much you love her and how much she turns you on. Send flowers for no reason. Meet her for a drink after work.

I have spoken with hundreds of couples in a Female Led Relationship, and many of the women admit that it is the actions of their men helping put them in the mood. Even though your woman is in charge, you are still committed to getting her relaxed, happy, and turned on to have mind-blowing sex. One ritual which must be avoided is sitting on the couch. On the night you are getting ready to worship your Queen, do anything you can to avoid sitting on the sofa watching TV. You want to draw her a bath, lay out her favorite lingerie, set the mood, and wait in the bedroom with candles, massage oil, and sex toys. She must be instructed to come to bed early so you can begin with a nice long massage and caressing. Sometimes a warm bath with candles and some wine can help get her in the mood. You will need to set this up for her. Make it a sweet surprise.

Refrain from eating a heavy dinner, so both of you can feel comfortable. Set the mood by beginning with touching her hair, kissing, massaging. Play her favorite music, use candles with sweet scents, and do everything with care. Remove all distractions—phones, laptops, and pets, and put the kids to bed. The setup is vitally important. Date night is another way to get in the mood. Get outside the house to have some fun before returning home to serve your Queen. Keep it interesting. Change it up. No one likes the same boring routine each week, and boredom is the kiss of death for relationships.

Transform Your Bedroom for Sex

1. Make Your Bedroom Off Limits

Kids, in-laws, parents, friends, and pets should not be allowed into your bedroom, and it should remain untouchable by the outside world. Here are some ways you can ensure this:

- Place a lock on your door.

- Put up blackout curtains.

- Keep your phones off and out of the room

- Make sure that there's no TV in the room

- Reserve your bedroom for sleep and for deeply connecting sexual intimacy.

2. Add Scents

Scented candles, flowers, and scents are all great ways to enhance your bedroom and make it sexy. Try various scents on different nights to spice things up. Whether you and your man want to relax after a busy day at the office, or you both use them to wake up and energize your senses for sex and spanking, scents can make all the difference.

Essential oil diffuser, some lightly scented candles, scents. and perfumes can all be great to enhance the mood. Make sure you choose them together.

3. Keep Your Bedroom at a Slightly Cooler Temperature

When it comes to the sexiness of your bedroom, the temperature definitely matters. If it's too cold, then it might limit the number of positions you can do, and the body does not warm up. If it's too hot, then it's uncomfortable for both of you. Sweating too much can kill the mood.

4. Massage Oils Are Fun

Sensual massage is one of the most efficient ways to get out of your head and into your body while simultaneously connecting with your partner and engaging in some light foreplay. Massage oils can be used in between spanking as well as before and after. It's a luxurious way to add to the sensations of the sessions.

5. Get Some Sexy Sheets

Nothing is a greater turn-on than some sexy sheets. Get a set of quality, high thread count sheets that you both will enjoy. Avoid buying white sheets because, believe it or not, stains are easily visible. Consider a sexy pattern or satin sheets so when you lie on them, they put you both in the mood.

6. Set Up a Great Music System

Music and sex both tap into very primal parts of our brain, which is why the two go so well together. It might sound like it has the potential to be cheesy, but don't knock it until you've tried it. The right music can add a whole new swagger to your mattress mambo. Choose whatever makes you feel the sexiest. Pick up a set of quality speakers and cue up your skillfully cultivated playlist, and let the sweet tunes carry you further into your body.

Every *Love & Obey* female led woman loves oral sex and enjoys it again and again. In fact, there are very few women on the planet who don't grow to absolutely enjoy oral sex done right. You are now challenged to become a master of giving it. You will be rewarded with a happy partner who will be so much more enthusiastic about sex. If you are single and in the dating world, learning how to dominate a woman in the bedroom with killer oral skills moves you up the ranks quickly.

You may find that you connect with your ideal woman much faster because your connection is so much deeper. Women will flock to you in the dating world because it's very difficult to find enthusiastic men. When men are able to fully satisfy a Goddess, relationships can be turned around.

Arousal Non-Concordance

Some couples can experience arousal non-concordance, which is mismatched arousal. Arousal non-concordance can occur when the brain and the body are out of sync. An example would be if you felt really turned on but had difficulty getting wet or erect or your body responded to a sexual stimulus, but your mind was saying no, then you've experienced arousal non-concordance.

Women tend to experience this when they love their men, but they are not sufficiently relaxed or turned on. Men can also feel affected and bothered as well because they feel lacking in their ability to arouse and stimulate. This is where Female Led Relationships and the importance of sex is for the Queen come in. The more men can focus on turning on the Queen throughout the day through their service, the better will be the sex when you are intimate.

In the preparation for sex, it is important to communicate and figure out what really turns us on or off and open up the conversation with each other. Maybe your Queen's mental desire for sex is present but she isn't feeling physically up to it, or she isn't enjoying certain positions. It may be time to get reacquainted with what can enhance arousal and take the time to think about what you like and don't like. If you experience physical arousal more than mental arousal, implementing something like a meditation practice or assessing what triggers your responsive desire can help your subjective arousal catch up to your physical response to sexual stimuli.

CHAPTER 9

How to Perform Oral Pleasure

When you are finally in bed ready to have sex, begin slowly and gently. Make sure she is in a comfortable position. Tell her you will be switching it up if you have not had oral sex for a long time. Get her in the mood first. I cannot stress the importance of this. Kiss her neck, her lips, her breasts, her chest, and her navel, making your way down. Savor each moment as though you are discovering her body for the first time. Tell her how beautiful she is, how much you love the feel of her curves and her skin. It's going to be so much more soothing when you keep the focus on your Queen at all times. Men often underestimate the power of a compliment. Now you are going to be performing oral sex like there is a real art to it.

While you are performing oral sex, you may have a lot of thoughts going through your mind. You may wonder, "Is she enjoying it?" "Am I doing this correctly?" Be confident and look for clues. Is she relaxed? Is she moaning? Is she smiling? If she isn't, ask questions: "How is this?" "Do you like this?"

In the beginning, it should be much more like you are teasing her. You're getting her excited. You're kissing outside her panties, then slowly slipping them off. Maintaining eye contact. Every movement and eye contact should be deliberate. You're watching her breathing, her noises, the look on her face. You are maintaining all the focus on her enjoyment. The idea is to slowly seduce her as you are getting her excited.

Now you are ready to give mind-blowing oral sex to your queen. Your focus should always be on how you can connect to the divine force and energy in her, how you can get her to come alive. One of the worst experiences I discussed with a man was regarding his wife, a gorgeous model, who lay on the bed, not making any sound or movement while he performed sex acts. I saw this as a huge problem, and I suggested that he needed to talk with her. You need to have open communication and feedback from your Goddess. If you cannot determine if she enjoys the sex or how she feels, you will need to request feedback directly. It's the only way you will learn and improve your skills.

One of the most important parts of foreplay is to place your Queen in a relaxed, happy positive mood. Queens can be apprehensive if they are new to oral pleasure and positive compliments help reassure her that you are eager and excited to please her. Tell her that her scent is provocative and turns you on. Once you get down there, stop for a moment and tell her that you love the way she tastes. Compliment that her pussy is fantastic, powerful, and you love everything about it. If you can convey each of these beliefs to her in a sincere way, you're going to be on your way to giving head and getting ahead.

Once you get down there, taking your time is another great way to help her feel more relaxed and excited about what you have in store for her. Begin slowly. Caress, massage, kiss, and draw out the initial contact. This is the foreplay. You want to ensure she is really in the mood. Too many men cut this short and get down to the vagina too fast. Women will never enjoy oral sex if the foreplay is rushed. Many times, this is the problem with intercourse. The foreplay is rushed, and she doesn't have time to relax, then it's "wham bam, thank you, ma'am." This is forbidden in oral sex. You need to give her time to build her divine energy, and you almost need to be going into your own state of euphoria as you get down to performing your mind-blowing oral sex on her.

After complimenting her, begin to move slowly down her stomach and thigh. Take your time kissing, hugging, touching, and even talking a little bit more about how going down on her has been a fantasy of yours and you're really excited. Make sure she's aroused before you dive in between her legs. Once you're down there, continue taking your time and start with light licks from the bottom of her pussy to the top. The clitoris is extremely sensitive, so you don't want to dive in right away. The reason why oral sex is so powerful is the clitoris. It is the main region of focus of oral sex for her, but you want to take your time getting there. The clitoris is the most nerve-rich part of a woman's body. The clitoral glans contain about eight thousand nerve endings, making it the powerhouse of pleasure.

To get some perspective, that's twice as many nerve endings as the penis. And its potential doesn't end there. This tiny erogenous zone spreads to fifteen thousand other nerves in the vagina area, which explains why women love oral sex so much. We know women are all unique, and the pussy is not any different, so every woman's pussy and even their clits are different. Every woman needs a different kind of stimulation to feel satisfied, depending on her unique biology. For some women, it's so sensitive that they may not want it to be stimulated directly. Some women may prefer touching near and around the clitoris but not directly on it because it is simply too sensitive with direct stimulation. Other women are fine with direct stimulation and even want you to suck on it until they orgasm.

Oh, and one more thing, we've all heard about the infamous G-spot. Maybe you've been confused about where it is or how to find it. This notorious pleasure zone became sensationalized back in the eighties when it was believed that if you could only access the G-spot inside the vagina, it would promote female orgasm. But now we know that some women have more sensitivity from the internal parts of the clitoral complex. That's why some women prefer vaginal penetration and intercourse more than other women. It may take a bit of time for you to learn how to stimulate all the right areas, but with practice comes perfection, which is why it is important to have regular sex and engage in oral sex with your Goddess as the focus. Anyone can slip the penis in and move back and forth until you orgasm. It takes a real Casanova to master giving great oral sex to a Queen.

There is also the opportunity to add sex toys. These can add lots of variation and excitement. The following are the best sex toys available for her. Vibrators are probably the most common type of sex toy. Wand vibrators are more intense with higher RPM. They can also be great massagers for the shoulders, legs, and back. Clitoral vibrators are typically much smaller and are best for people who like direct clitoral stimulation.

Dildos are meant to simulate penile penetration. They can be any length or girth. There are ones that are two inches and ones that are monster-sized. People who enjoy the feeling of being penetrated or like the feeling of fullness in their vagina or anus might enjoy dildo play. Be careful when using sex toys, though. Master your technique of oral first, and then add them in as a side dish. Make sure you don't upset the whole experience by trying to make the sex toy the focus and make sure she is comfortable with the use of the toy. As with everything, personal hygiene and cleaning of sex toys directly after use are recommended.

Butt plugs stimulate the ring of nerves around the anus. The difference between using a butt plug and using a dildo is where a dildo goes in and out, the butt plug just stays in and gives a sustained feeling of fullness. The rabbit toy is a combo of an external vibrator and a G-spot toy. It has an external part that usually looks like rabbit ears that provides vibration to the clitoris. And a second attachment goes inside the vagina for G-spot stimulation, so you get double the sensation. Anal beads are another interesting toy.

Unlike butt plugs, which typically go in and stay in, anal beads provide the sensation of the anal sphincter opening and closing. Pulling them out as you orgasm can create a more intense orgasm.

CHAPTER 10

How to Deal with Hesitations About Oral Pleasure

Oral sex is growing and becoming more popular, so much so that it is now depicted very often in mainstream media, but women can still be hesitant about experiencing oral sex because of a variety of issues. How you handle these hesitations will dramatically affect your sex life.

Many women have convinced themselves that they don't like oral sex, and often they will try to convince their man of it too. There are also many instances of men wanting to give oral sex, but they do not know how to approach the subject or where to begin. Previously, you may have been unsure of your technique and worried about even doing it for fear of criticism from your Goddess. But all of these are just reasons based on insecurity. Once a woman feels comfortable letting you go down on her, everything changes, but the insecurities may take some time to address.

To begin with, research shows that issues over body image for both men and women are growing. When most people think of body image, they think about physical appearance and how attractive they are. But *Psychology Today* suggests that body image is our mental representation of ourselves and influences behavior, feelings, beliefs, plans, who we choose as a partner, our work, and our day-to-day interactions. So, the more that you, as the supportive gentleman, can influence your Queen's outlook and how she perceives herself, the more relaxed and happier she will be.

Women always complain of not feeling like their man truly appreciates them or finds them sexy. Women often compare themselves to other women, because deep down, they consider them to be competition. But what if your Queen had you reassuring her daily that she is supreme and that you only care about one thing: bringing her as much pleasure as possible. How would that change things for both of you? How would it transform your relationship?

Research shows that 56 percent of women are unhappy with their overall appearance—their abs and stomach, body weight, hips, and muscle. What was even more shocking was 63 percent of men also had issues with overall appearance, and similar to women, they were unhappy with their abs, chest, and muscle. Why is this important? Well, much of our behavior stems from these deep-seated issues with body image. I can recall my own experiences with being overweight and never feeling like I was good enough to be having sex with a man. I remember wearing heavy shapewear and being very paranoid when it came time for a man to discover what was under all of my clothes. I feel that it was this insecurity that may have driven me to the opposite spectrum of working out until I resembled an Olympic athlete.

Similarly, you and your Queen may be harboring some of these issues, and it is important to address and overcome them in a positive manner. Serving your Queen and accepting everything about her is the first step. Critical men immediately put the woman on the defensive, and an unhappy woman means an unhappy life and sex life. A woman is much less likely to be interested in regular sex, much less experimenting with oral sex, different positions, toys, and props.

How a woman feels about her body and how she thinks you think about her body will make a huge difference in how relaxed she is during sex to enjoy it. So, your job will entail bolstering her ego and how she feels each and every day. You can tell her how beautiful she is, how much you love her stomach, breasts, thighs. You should be flirty throughout the day, not just during foreplay. Go shopping with her, help her choose sexy clothing, and be open when she expresses her insecurities. "Honey, how does my butt look in these jeans?" should be met with, "You're gorgeous," or "You look incredible." Some women may disagree with this approach, but women are suckers for flattery. That said, how you treat your Queen should never be fake or false. A smart sophisticated woman will always know if you are lying.

Psychology Today research reveals that 89 percent of women wanted to lose weight. They also found that more than 57 percent felt inadequate in their twenties, which is when many relationships begin to form. Forty percent of women also indicated that their partner's opinion of their appearance was extremely important to body image. So, chances are, your Goddess could be unhappy with her body and will need some reassurance from you. Many women indicate that if their partner sees them as beautiful, they are more likely to feel beautiful and rely less on their own criticism. This is an opportunity for you not only to be a great lover but a great partner.

Part of being a great partner is showing unconditional support to your Goddess and accepting her for all of her strengths and weaknesses. The more you can do this in daily life, the more it spills over into your sex life. Research shows that twice as many people judge sexual experiences as a source of good feelings rather than bad. For both sexes, interpersonal and emotional factors more often serve to reinforce, not punish. This is encouraging news; it implies that there are many avenues for us to improve our feelings about our bodies.

There is no doubt that sexual experiences affect our body image, and our body image affects our sex. The less attractive you or your Queen feel, the less likely you are to enjoy the sexual experience and the less relaxed she will feel about opening up to oral sex. This affects you too since 70 percent of men say that sexual experience affects their general life and their self-image. The moral of the story is that there are so many factors that can affect your relationship and your sex life, so open communication is the best way to solve many of the issues which often lead to the negativity which eventually leads to the destruction of relationships.

Let's investigate the psychology of why women are still against oral sex and how you can help to change this. When a woman feels confident in her look, taste, and scent down there, she will even enjoy kissing her man after he goes down there. She will enjoy tasting what he just tasted and enjoy sharing the taste on his lips and her lips together after an extra wet oral sex session.

When I was working on this book, I discovered that quite a few women were very uncomfortable and got no pleasure from receiving oral sex. They are uptight about it and don't like having their men down there. They don't even understand why a man would like to go down on a woman. If they reluctantly agreed to it, they allowed it because they thought their men liked it. Even then, the women would lie passively and wait, enduring it with no pleasure until the end. I wondered how these women could not realize how great oral sex can be. I had experienced all of these incredible orgasms from it, and I couldn't imagine living without it.

Most women are lucky enough to orgasm during an initial oral sex experience. These fortunate women experience some early pleasure and learn to improve the experience each time. As a result, they increase the quality and quantity of their orgasms by naturally testing and trying different techniques and positions until they create their unique style of receiving and orgasming from oral sex. So not only do you as a man need to learn the basic techniques and positions in this book, but you need to pay attention to each woman. You have to be sensitive to each woman's style of receiving.

Some women even discover the pleasure of oral sex for the first time with another female during high school or college experimentation with girl-on-girl sex. They may test their lesbian or bisexual tendencies by taking a walk on the wild side with a lesbian friend or a bi-curious college roommate. Most lesbian and bisexual women are more than happy to help a heterosexual woman experiment. Lesbians and bi women are also enthusiastic and excited about an invitation to have sex with another woman—and that enthusiasm is a key turn-on in the oral sex arena.

If you do try it, paraphrasing Katy Perry's famous song "I Kissed a Girl," you just might say, "I tried going down on a girl, and I liked it," and after that, you will probably love giving it as much as getting it. But if talking your woman into a bisexual experience is a little more than you think she would be willing to do, then you will have to show her that you are eager to please her down there and offer some serious compliments. As I explained earlier in the Oral Sex by Numbers sections of this book, the point of all this is that most women have to learn how to orgasm from oral sex; it does not come automatically.

So, you must seduce her into it by being very excited and enthusiastic about going down on her. Once you get down there and give her first oral orgasm, her opinions about oral sex will quickly change, trust me. The biggest part of this whole problem comes from the media and advertising. Millions of dollars go into douche and tampon commercials in magazines, TV, and online. Growing up, women are taught our vaginas are nasty and dirty, stemming from decades of patriarchal conditioning and lack of research. It's horrible, but the misogynist, patriarchal-based religions and social teachings of the past few centuries have tried to convince us that the female sex organ is filthy, which we now know is medically false.

In fact, a normal healthy vagina is the cleanest place in the body. It is even cleaner than the mouth. But still, our discomfort remains, and for so many reasons. However, this social conditioning has caused millions of women to have low opinions of their pussies. They think they are smelly and gross. This same social conditioning causes many women to have a stigma against lesbians. They think lesbians are gross because they love to put their faces in pussies.

Women feel uncomfortable about the way their pussies look, smell, and taste due to being socially conditioned since they were young that it is dirty down there. It is really tragic that society would promote such a bald-faced lie simply to keep women down and destroy their self-esteem. You can actually be part of the *Love & Obey* movement, guys. You can start reconditioning your women that their pussies are beautiful. Whether your woman has more, less, or no hair, two big plump outer mounds, a set of uneven inner lips, a big or small clit, you have to love every inch of it. So, if your woman is wondering why you want to put your face between her legs and lick, kiss, and suck her down there, you need to convince her that her pussy is beautiful, smells great, and tastes delicious, and that it really turns you on to be close to her. Enthusiasm will get you everywhere.

CHAPTER 11

Rules of a Female Led Relationship

The rules of a Female Led Relationship are established to ensure you have guidelines on how to thrive in your relationship.

Here are some guidelines that need to be followed:

1. **Understanding roles and boundaries.** Both partners need to be comfortable and happy with the setup of a relationship. The best way for this to happen is that the roles in the relationship are clear, and both partners accept their roles and know where boundaries are drawn. Communication about who will take care of responsibilities and clearly outlining duties and roles for both of you is crucial. You want to ensure that you are both on the same page before you dive into female led life. Once roles and boundaries are established, there are fewer arguments.

2. **Transparency and honesty.** For any relationship, transparency, and honesty are both so important. You and your partner should feel comfortable approaching each other if there are issues with the setup of the

relationship. Both you and your Queen need to feel heard and free to express their feelings and concerns. I always suggest that couples have a discussion hour once a week when an open discussion is encouraged. Sunday evening or morning over brunch is ideal, so you start the week off right. You and your Queen take turns to discuss the relationship, your experiences, desires, issues, and hesitations. Refrain from being critical and never interrupt your Queen when she is speaking.

3. **Review the relationship.** It is very rare that two people know exactly what they want. A Female Led Relationship might be working now, but it might not be what works forever. Take the time to review your relationship periodically, making sure everyone is happy. If you are following the weekly discussion period, this can be very helpful. Otherwise, once every few weeks is mandatory to discuss your relationship.

4. **Remember the love.** A Female Led Relationship isn't about power, but it is a structure for two people who love each other to choose to follow. Don't fall into the trap of being more concerned with your role than what you actually feel for your partner. Make decisions because you love each other. Focus on the love and the connection you have built. Sometimes we take for granted our relationships or marriages, and we fail to see the bigger picture. It is important to remember the love and the real reasons you are together.

5. **Ignore opinions.** One thing that stays constant is everyone has an opinion. But what's right for one couple may not work for others. Ignore the critics. You and your Queen know what's best for your lives. Don't allow the opinions and criticisms of others to hinder your exploration and what you and your Queen decide

to pursue. Self-acceptance has become a popular theme today, and this applies to relationships as well. Accept your limitations and be honest about strengths and weaknesses and communicate about them. No other person can comment on what works for you and your Queen, so be true to your own goals and desires.

The Queen's Rules for Her Supportive Gentleman

1. The Queen makes the rules.

2. Your Queen creates a list of rules, chores, and regulations for you to follow. They should be reviewed regularly together. This helps to set the expectations and parameters of the relationship.

3. Establish yourself as a masculine "Knight" figure. She will be your Queen and you are her knight, which means your purpose in life is to support her and be at her side. You should address her as "Queen," "Mistress," and "Goddess" as much as possible.

4. Be respectful of her wishes and desires at all times, even when you disagree. Allow her to express her views and listen intently. This is not always easy for men, as you will want to go into a defensive, guarded, and silent position when confronted. Generally, women want to be heard, and they often need a good listener. So, be that confidant for her—someone who she can discuss any issue openly.

5. Keep up with your chores without the need for constant reminders. If she decides that your duties are taking out the garbage and doing the dishes, do them each day without having to be reminded. Your goal is to reduce her responsibility with the domestic chores. Feel free to add some chores and surprise her from time to time.

6. Be attractive to your Queen. Try to present yourself the way she prefers. If she likes a beard or goatee, then try to grow it. If she prefers a lean muscular body, then try to lose weight and tone up. The idea is that you must be attractive to each other to keep the attraction alive. This is more important for you, her submissive, as you follow the rules she makes. Just because she is in charge does not release her of the same responsibility to keep the sexiness alive.

7. In a Female Led Relationship, the number one rule is sex is for the Queen's pleasure, so you will need to ensure you are well prepared with tips and techniques on how to turn her on. Do you know how to pleasure her properly? If your skills are not up to her standards, then get my book *Oral Sex for Women* and brush up on your skills. Are you a great lover? Do you switch things up, change up your technique for intercourse, oral sex, and foreplay? Knowing how to pleasure your Queen is mandatory.

8. Engage in discussions about your fantasies and what really turns her on. If you've been with your Queen for years, there might be all sorts of sexual fantasies that she has waiting for you both to explore. Since everything requires mutual consent, it will be important for both of you to be completely honest about your wants and desires.

9. Your Queen makes the decisions about sex. She decides when, where, and how you have sex. She may decide to put you in chastity or demand that you come only when she commands. You are free to add some ideas but generally, you will obey her. If she wants oral sex, you perform it. If she wants kissing and foreplay all night, the answer is the same: "Yes, my Queen." You ask her when you want to orgasm: May I orgasm tonight? You never ever ejaculate on her face, body, or anywhere else unless she gives you her consent. If she wants to give you fellatio, she decides

how long and if she does it at all. It should never be assumed. You will ask her how she wants to be pleasured each day. These are things you will need to discuss with her in an open conversation. If your Queen forbids you from masturbating, you must stop. This is the difference with a Female Led Relationship—you must take your orders from her. Any argument and objections mean you are not really practicing FLR. Now, does this mean there is no mutual consent? Absolutely not. You must voice any and all concerns. You both need to encourage open and honest communication.

10. Compliment your Queen, and flattery will get you everywhere. You and your Queen are the only ones who can pump each other up, and for your Queen to be inspired to take on the leadership role, she will need plenty of encouragement from you. Men often reveal that they never feel compelled to compliment their partners because they should already know that the man loves her, but human beings need to be reassured, and your Queen needs to hear that you appreciate and love her each and every day.

11. Most men think women don't want sex as much until they meet one who does. Your biggest problem will come from keeping up with her unleashed desires. The truth is that many women don't want sex often because they are not being satisfied by selfish untrained men. When you focus on her pleasure—and she is thoroughly enjoying and participating in sex—you'll see her new sexy side, and her appetite for sex may become unsatiable. It's like letting the Genie out of the bottle. She won't be restrained again anytime soon.

When you start focusing 100 percent on her pleasure, and she knows that sex is for her enjoyment, she will want it much more often.

12. Becoming the right partner and getting plenty of practice will help you learn to become comfortable enough in your skin to fully appreciate the wonder that is the oral orgasm. Learning to make her feel good will make you a better man and more confident, which ultimately will make you more likely to feel satisfied. Needless to say, the more often you experience orally pleasuring your Queen, the more quickly you'll achieve the female led attitude that your pleasure comes from giving pleasure. Your pleasure will come from orgasming her as much as possible, and you will have an unbelievable sense of satisfaction. The goal of your intimacy should be to satisfy both of you, placing the focus on her first.

13. Your Queen will probably want to take control over the finances and your earnings. Female led women are usually strong capable women, and they often want to control the finances. Your Queen may decide to leave you in control of the money, otherwise, she may give you an allowance and take control of it all. This does not mean you won't make decisions together about major purchases of how to handle taxes, etc. On the contrary—both of you can feel like you have a voice in what happens. All too often in traditional relationships, men control the finances, and they may or may not be adept and successful in financial management. When women control the finances, she feels a greater sense of authority and power, and you naturally become more submissive and obedient. I feel that it is also a great indicator of trust you will need to have in her ability to lead the family.

14. When it comes to social activities, your Queen makes the final decision and sets the schedule of activities for the family. She decides where you will go, on what days, and what events and activities are appropriate for the kids. But you must also offer your input in a respectful manner. For

example, if going to the movies, the Queen decides what to watch, where to sit, and the type of snacks to eat and drink. If she decides to allow you to make decisions, it is still up to you to ask what she wants and to get it. The idea is that you surrender to her decisions, but you support her by taking care of things and offering your help. All too often, I witness women dragging bags from shopping or having to get all of the family snacks, stumbling over people in a theater with no help from her partner. It is the opposite in a Female Led Relationship, and you are supporting her every step of the way.

15. Obedience 24/7/365 is the foundation of any FLR. Discipline is, therefore, a necessary element of the relationship to ensure you comply with your Queen's wishes. Verbal discipline is the way I choose to ensure obedience but physical discipline is also part of the teaching if it suits the *Love & Obey* Queen. Disobedience will be met with strict discipline and punishment. Your Queen may prefer physical punishment such as spanking or slapping. This can be sexy spanking and even more regular spankings to ensure discipline on a daily basis. No matter the choice, you and your Queen must discuss all boundaries and limits. Yes, you must obey her, but everything must be done with consent.

If your Queen requires amusement, you do it. I might order my man to crawl on the floor, kiss my feet, and then "hee-haw" like a jackass. I find it a very amusing punishment, and it gets the point across to him in a harmless and painless way that he was acting like an ass. Some men object to this, yet this was exactly a very memorable scene in the movie *9½ Weeks*. She had to crawl for her man, and there were no objections raised by men or women at this time. So, this is the type of double standard that no longer exists in a Female Led Relationship.

CHAPTER 12

Chastity and the Female Led Relationship

C hastity has become one of the biggest categories of interest in Female Led Relationships, and it's exploded in the last five years. There are more TV shows and scenes in movies depicting it, and if you search the chastity cage on Amazon, you'll see thousands of brands and devices available for sale. One brand reported over a million devices sold in the last twelve months, which means that millions of couples are obsessed with chastity. Chastity is searched 200,000 times a month on Google. Why all the fascination?

What is chastity, and why is interest in it growing exponentially? Couples have reported that chastity and orgasm control has transformed their relationship or marriage, injecting excitement, adventure, and taking intimacy to a whole new level. Who would think that millions of men would crave wearing a chastity lock for days with their Queen holding the only key?

That's real trust and devotion. Chastity means abstinence. The man refrains from sexual intercourse or having an orgasm unless the Queen gives him permission. At first glance, this may seem like the most unnatural thing in the world. Some may even think, why would I want to stop my man's orgasm? This was my first thought when I was introduced to it, but after my experience and an in-depth analysis, the true power of male chastity was revealed.

Today, chastity has become a transformative experience for many relationships. At the source, and an important point for women to understand, when a man agrees to chastity, he is showing complete submission and devotion to his Queen, over and above any other undertaking in life. In addition, it gives the woman complete control over him. This is the ultimate sign of respect to the Queen and is essentially what transforms the relationship.

As part of a Female Led Relationship, male chastity becomes the major test, and many couples have reported much more intimacy and a deepening of their bond after starting chastity. Male chastity may take many forms: using a physical locking device, the chastity cage, or none at all. It may involve orgasm control, semen ejaculation control, or simply no sexual gratification at all. Some men remain locked for hours, some for days. The length of time is determined by the Queen, but like all other practices in the relationship, there must still be consent from both partners.

Chastity is not to be used as a way to punish the man. The real reason for chastity is to deepen the man's fixation on the Queen as the ultimate ruler of the relationship. She who holds the key to his lock has the ultimate control. As a sexual practice in the female led lifestyle, male chastity, in my opinion, is the crème de la crème. The Queen has the ultimate control, and she is the supreme leader.

For men in a Female Led Relationship or crave being in one, giving the Queen this kind of control will be orgasmic in itself. It takes your arousal, sex, and daily life to a whole new level. It requires some sacrifice, but the relationship is transformed and both of you will evolve.

More couples have admitted to engaging in chastity and making it the focus in their relationships. Statistics don't lie. Male chastity is part of Female Led Relationships, and as the leader of the Love & Obey Female Led Movement, I can confirm that interest in a female taking the lead and the man becoming the supportive gentleman is expanding worldwide. Men contact me every day and ask questions about how to serve their Queen correctly.

My five bestselling books are all geared to help couples wake up a dead marriage and inject some new life and purpose into relationships. Today, chastity takes female led to a whole new level. In a Female Led Relationship, the desire to be controlled by a strong female becomes even more important. More women are taking control of many aspects of their lives, and many are leading countries, governments, corporations, cities, households, and now the bedroom. Part of keeping the relationship spark alive is controlling the focus of the man's desire on the Queen.

Every woman knows that men are driven by sex. It's natural for them. It is a primitive urge that's impossible for men to ignore. It is programmed in their DNA from the dawn of time. The irresistible force of their libido is like a raging fire, burning up everything that stands in the way of its desire to consume. When you are in a relationship, the Queen becomes the object of his desire. As part of a Female Led Relationship, controlling a man's orgasm is the ultimate control, and this could be why male chastity is growing exponentially.

Why do men crave chastity? I believe that it goes back to their need for attention from a strong female. Fifty percent of marriages will end in divorce, which means a significant part of the population will be raised by women. Of the households with two-parent families, many are experiencing a shift where the woman assumes control. So, children, particularly men, will crave a strong dominant female like their mothers. "Men marry their mothers" refers to the idea that more men will choose a long-term partner who exhibits similar characteristics and may even resemble their mothers. I also believe that men crave the same discipline and attention they received from a strong maternal figure. The Queen who places her man in chastity has the ultimate control, and men love this. They succumb to a strong female because it keeps the focus on them. More focus on the relationship means a stronger relationship or marriage.

In Female Led Relationships, more men have admitted that they enjoy and have a strong desire for their women to control them. For instance, placing a penis into a chastity lock where the Queen has the only key is arousing in itself. Today, more relationships are being led by women. Women are taking charge in the household and in the bedroom. Men are loving the experience of being under the spell and the dominance of women and spanking adds to the feeling of control for the Queen. When women feel empowered, they are at their best, and men get excited when they take charge and show their power. It's a win-win for most.

CHAPTER 13

Why Is Chastity Such a Turn-On?

M ale chastity involves giving complete control to your Queen, and she ultimately makes all of the decisions. Why is it such a turn-on? The Queen holds the key to the chastity device, and she controls orgasm. To understand what happens with male chastity, and why it's such a turn-on, it's important to look at what happens at a physiological level. Below, we will analyze the sexual response cycle.

There are four stages in the sexual response cycle:

1. Desire: The initial excitement phase is triggered by mental or physical stimuli with increased muscle tension, erect nipples, blood flow to genitals, vaginal lubrication, and pre-cum.

2. Arousal: This is the plateau phase with heightened sexual tension and sensitivity just before orgasm.

3. Orgasm: This is the forceful release of sexual tension resulting in muscle contractions and ejaculation; generally, only lasting a few seconds up to a minute.

4. Resolution: This is the state of recovery and the return to a normal state. Penises refract, but continued stimulation in some vaginas can lead to multiple orgasms.

The desire phase is the first stage, and this is where there is an increase in muscle tension, blood flow to the genitals, erect nipples, and vaginal lubrication. Things are getting heated up, and arousal begins. The arousal phase is where breathing, heart rate, and blood pressure significantly increase. The woman's clitoris becomes highly sensitive, the man's testicles retract into the scrotum, and muscle spasms may begin in the feet, face, and hands.

It is here that orgasm denial can begin. You can start by teasing and denying any touching or further arousal. Keeping your partner at the height of their arousal phase for longer—without letting them reach the orgasm phase—can be enjoyable for both of you. This represents one type of chastity.

Once you have satisfied your tease and denial, it's time for the orgasm phase. This is typically the shortest of all the phases and consists of muscle contractions and ejaculation. In chastity, the Queen can deny the orgasm altogether or prolong it as long as possible. Following an orgasm, the resolution phase allows the body to slowly return to its normal state. This phase often accompanies feelings of satisfaction, intimacy, and fatigue. If no more stimulation follows an orgasm, this phase will begin immediately. The brain releases a variety of chemicals when we feel lust and attraction. Lust stimulates the production of estrogen and testosterone in the body, which increases erotic feelings and behavior.

When feeling attracted to another person, our dopamine levels surge, which is the same chemical produced when we feel good, for instance, during sexual stimulation. The more you lust and want an orgasm, the more of these chemicals circulating to keep you focused on the object of your attention, which is the Queen who holds the key to your orgasm. It is these physiological responses that make chastity so powerful because ultimately the man's whole physiological response during sex is controlled by the Queen.

Chastity is a turn-on because it immediately injects a sense of excitement and sexual tension into the relationship each and every day. When both partners are engaged and focused on each other, with the Queen teasing and the man showing complete willpower and devotion by holding back the most powerful urge in the body, this creates a continuous feeling of heightened sexuality. Each day is exhilarating, rather than a feeling of boredom and monotony. Chastity is the furthest thing from boring, and it helps to refocus the couple's energy on themselves, which increases intimacy, communication, and connection in the relationship.

As a woman, the ultimate sign of control is to put a cage on your man. Even if it seems like fun and a distraction, it still centers the attention on him. In turn, he shows complete devotion to you as he is now yours. He submits to you controlling his every move. He can't go far and roam free with you having locked up his penis, and since you are the person who will hold the key to his freedom, you become his ultimate Queen, Goddess, and ruler. This control of a man's manhood is a major turn-on for them.

The great philosopher Hegel said in his master-slave dialectic, "Desire plays a very important role." This philosopher stated that animals have a desire that is satisfied with an immediate object. The animal isn't aware of what it desires. However, this is different for human beings. For Hegel, history equals the history of social relations—two human desires are facing each other. What human beings really desire is to be desired by others.

In other words, they want to be recognized by others. This means that human desire is fundamentally a yearning for recognition. Human beings want others to give them an autonomous value—a value that's their own and makes them different from others. This is what defines the human condition.

Therefore, according to Hegel, the main characteristic of human beings is imposing themselves on others. This is why male chastity—with the Queen imposing her will on a man and all the focus is on him while he desires her and is turned on by her controlling him—is so powerful. It goes to the heart of the social condition. The desire part, like Hegel proposes, is a fundamental need for human beings.

Since the beginning of history, there have been dominators and dominated people. Due to that dominance, the master coerces the slave and forces him or her to work. However, the master ends up depending on the slave to be able to survive. But what is important here is that even though the master is in control and holds the power, the slave is indispensable. This applies to Female Led Relationships and chastity because many opponents will argue that the Queen has all the power, but in fact, it is the man who becomes invaluable as he serves her. She needs him more now, and he fulfills his position as the supportive gentleman.

Chastity takes this even further in the desire component. The basic human need is fulfilled, and the desire for the Queen and her desire to be served is what makes this so powerful for relationships. In my experience, it has the power to transform the relationship in ways, which could not be achieved by counseling, retreats, or any other method.

Remember, power can be defined as the ability or capacity to direct or influence the behavior of others in a particular way. Power is not limited to domination and submission.

Instead, power in relationships is understood to be the respective abilities of each person in the relationship to influence each other and direct the relationship—and this is a very complex element of romantic partnerships that are changing every day. More men want their women to have power over them. In same-sex relationships, one partner always dominates.

CHAPTER 14

Types of Male Chastity

E rotic sexual denial and male orgasm control is one of the major forms of chastity. They involve the act of experiencing or allowing someone else to experience a high level of sexual arousal and pleasure for a long time without allowing an orgasm. This can be done with or without a male chastity device. For many, orgasm control is about the physical build-up and release. For others, the psychological aspect of power, control, and giving in is the hotness.

A submissive man is obedient and will do anything possible to not come until the dominant Queen gives permission or forces the orgasm. If the submissive isn't strong enough to hold the orgasm on their own, the Queen can stop the orgasm simply with a command. The fantasy of being controlled usually drives the intensity of the orgasm, coupled with anticipation and release that typically increases the strength of how the partner experiences the orgasm.

Orgasm control of your man allows you, the Queen, to experience a high level of sexual arousal and pleasure for a long time along with multiple orgasms while not allowing the man any pleasure except the gratification he receives from pleasuring his woman. Over time, this trains the man to focus on the female's pleasure and be grateful for permission to ejaculate once in a while. It's an area of erotic experience for many in Female Led Relationships. Orgasm control also involves erotic sexual denial in which he is kept in a heightened state of sexual arousal for an extended length of time without being allowed an orgasm.

Erotic sexual denial has the power to strengthen your intimacy with your man and lead both of you to higher levels of sexual stimulation without allowing him to orgasm. In Female Led Relationships, the Queen is in charge and has all of the power to control her man. So, taking a dominant role and holding off his ejaculation for an extended time frame will give him toe-curling orgasms when you do finally take them over the edge and allow him to orgasm. Deliberately holding your man back from that explosive moment will lead to amplified erotic fantasies about you and heighten his anticipation of finally being unlocked and having sex with you—you will become his sex Goddess.

Erotic sexual denial can last for short periods or long periods, or it may be used for those who really enjoy drawing out the anticipation of sexual intercourse until all other tasks or sexual acts are completed. Your man can remain locked at all times when all you desire is orgasming with oral sex stimulation. The only time to unlock your man is when you want penetration and the special satisfaction gained from sexual intercourse. All other times keep him locked, which can be minutes, days, weeks, or even months, depending on your sexual desires. If you've been dying for more oral ladies, male chastity is one of the greatest ways to achieve this.

Every man needs to experience erotic orgasm denial. Prolonging that urge for an extended period of time can lead to dramatic amounts of sexual arousal and excitement. Prolonging the man's urge to explode goes a long way to helping the Queen to not only demonstrate her ultimate control, but he is trained to have willpower and self-control. The Queen becomes a supreme leader when she controls the driving force in a man.

Even in infidelity, most men are not out just looking for pure sex. If this were the case, most men would be seeking a prostitute. When a man cheats, he is searching for that excitement and desire missing from his current relationship. With male chastity, the Queen can control his desire just by controlling his penis and his ability to have orgasms. So male chastity can also be used as a tool to wake up a dead sex life and refocus the spotlight back on the Queen.

Types of Orgasm Control

Orgasm control can also involve additional practices like edging, peaking, or surfing, and they are different from male orgasm denial. Although orgasm and ejaculation are delayed, they are eventually allowed at the end of each of these types of orgasm control. Orgasm denial prohibits men from ejaculating without the female partner's permission; however, edging is where you bring your man right to the "edge"—the brink of orgasm, only to stop or slow down stimulation before reaching the climax.

You are not completely denying the orgasm, you are prolonging the entire experience. Edging can be done through clitoral and genital stimulation, prostate massage, blowjob intercourse, or other various sexual acts—whatever gets your arousal into overload. Rile him up over and over until you finally allow him to let go. It will be intensely erotic for both partners and often leads to feeling a much more intense and high-level orgasm.

Men become better versions of themselves when they are no longer constrained by selfish, male-focused, patriarchal sex. Once he can focus his attention on pleasing you, the Queen, every day of his life, he has a new purpose in life. He can work on succeeding at serving you, and that will only work to make you happier and increase the success of your marriage or Female Led Relationship. Think of how much fun it's going to be when every sex session is controlled and both of you are exploring raising arousal and your sexual enjoyment.

Avoid Masturbation

No masturbation and watching porn are the simplest, and therefore perhaps the easiest first step in male chastity and orgasm control as well as semen retention. A well-trained man in chastity needs to learn to avoid both orgasms and ejaculation from masturbation while you administer more training during your sex sessions. This is one of the most important steps in male chastity. Uncontrolled masturbation is simply not allowed and must be restrained if men are to experience the real power of male chastity. Orgasms and even semen are for the Queen only and not to be wasted with random sessions watching porn on his computer.

Not only does masturbating while on the computer decrease his time focusing on you, but most men can become addicted, and they can eventually affect the sensitivity of his penis to arousal methods. This is similar to women addicted to their vibrators. Pretty soon, no amount of human methods can satisfy genitals that have been overstimulated with external methods. As a western society, we have allowed this to go on unchecked, but in male chastity, the foundation is to build self-control and submit to the woman's command.

Pull-Out Method

The pull-out method is considered yet another form of orgasm control, in which immediately before the man orgasms, he pulls his penis out of the vagina just before ejaculation. This was traditionally used as a method for birth control, but it is part of semen retention and thought of as orgasm control. As you will see later in the *Love & Obey* method of orgasm control, he pulls out, then performs oral sex on you until you orgasm.

Semen Retention

Semen retention is yet another form of male chastity and orgasm control. Not only can the orgasm be denied, but so too can ejaculation be avoided either through sexual abstinence or by practicing intercourse without ejaculation. Semen retention does not refer to the avoidance of male pleasure. In this practice, male pleasure is separated from ejaculation, making it possible for the man to enjoy the full pleasure of sexual intercourse without experiencing seminal ejaculation. Semen retention is an ancient practice believed to maximize male physical and spiritual energy. Much of the history appears to be rooted in Taoism.

Worldwide, this practice exists in many cultures, under different names. Practitioners attribute near-mystical superpower qualities to semen conservation, and the men who practice orgasm control rave about its benefits. They experience a notable boost in courage and self-confidence. More energy and focus and an increased attractiveness to women. This makes it a contributor to male chastity, because again, the focus is on the Queen.

Some men claim to have greater mental clarity and awareness. And the motivation to do activities that are good for men like going to the gym, losing weight, increasing muscle mass, and sleeping better. They also claim to be more grounded and calmer. They say it boosts their sex drive, including harder erections, and they lose any erectile dysfunction that they had experienced.

CHAPTER 15

Physiological Effects of Chastity

T he power of male chastity and orgasm control comes from the many physiological changes that occur in the body. There are scientifically based health benefits for men from orgasm denial and semen conservation. The five scientifically measurable areas of impact on men are an increase in testosterone levels, an increase in brain androgen receptors, a decrease in dopamine levels, a decrease in prolactin levels, and an increase in serotonin levels. The most scientifically provable result of orgasm denial is an increase in testosterone. In the 1950s, Alfred Kinsey, the first scientist to study human sexuality in detail, described the orgasm as "an explosive discharge of neuromuscular tension."

The male orgasm is a complex system involving multiple hormones, organs, and nerve pathways. The hormone testosterone, which is produced in the testicles, plays a central role by enhancing the sexual desire libido that leads to arousal, erection, and ultimately orgasm. By contrast, low testosterone not only decreases a man's energy and mood, but it also makes him less responsive to sexual stimuli, both physical and mental.

A man often only requires physical stimulation to achieve arousal, while women typically need physical and mental stimulation to achieve the same. Men differ from women in that their orgasms, the climax of the sexual response, come on faster and are shorter than women.

Ejaculation is a complicated process. According to Healthline, here's a quick breakdown:

The physical stimulation of sexual contact sends signals through the central nervous system to the spinal cord and brain.

This stimulation continues until you reach the plateau phase in the sexual cycle, which leads up to orgasm.

Tubes in the testicles that store and move sperm (the vas deferens) squeeze sperm out of the testicles into the urethra at the bottom of the penis.

The prostate gland and seminal vesicles produce fluid that will carry the sperm out of the shaft as semen. This then gets rapidly ejaculated out of the penis. Muscles near the bottom of the penis continue to squeeze the penis tissues another five times or so to keep pushing semen out. The refractory period happens right after you orgasm. It lasts until you're able to get sexually aroused again. The refractory period varies from person to person. A variety of factors affect it, such as your age and overall health.

As you age, it may take longer to get aroused and ejaculate. It may take between 12 to 24 hours between arousal and ejaculation. This timing differs for everyone. Studies show sexual function changes most drastically around 40 years old.

No Ejaculation and Increased Testosterone

Research on the relationship between ejaculation and serum testosterone levels in men who masturbated every day for a week determined that when men don't masturbate for seven days, their testosterone levels increase by a whopping 45.7 percent. The significant testosterone increase could explain the purported physical benefits listed above and others, including a deeper voice, thicker hair, weight loss, greater strength, and power.

It may also explain some of the psychological benefits, including increased energy and focus, increased courage, self-confidence, and by correlation, the testosterone boost could even be the reason that men perceived themselves to be more attractive to women when they did not orgasm.

Frequent Masturbation Decreases Androgen Receptors

But testosterone requires androgen receptors. Androgen receptors allow your body to use testosterone, such as to develop a deep voice and other manly traits. Without androgen receptors, testosterone is useless. Frequent masturbation hasn't been completely proven yet to affect testosterone levels; however, overly active sexual activity like frequent masturbation has been proven, at least in lab mice, to significantly reduce the amount of androgen receptors in the body. It also boosts estrogen receptors and takes at least 15 days of abstinence to reverse these brain changes.

If a man constantly masturbates or orgasms, two events happen simultaneously. Dopamine plummets, and prolactin soars. Dopamine is "go for the pussy!" and prolactin is "take a break!" This mechanism shifts a man's attention from sex to hunting and gathering, taking care of babies, building shelters, and so forth. Without this natural shutdown, men would, and God help us, pursue sex to the exclusion of all other activities 24/7.

In the study, androgen receptors participate in the neuroendocrine regulation of male sexual behavior, primarily in brain areas located in the limbic system. It regulates the relationship between sexual satiety and motivation, brain androgen receptors. And testosterone in men creates a long-term inhibition of sexual behavior after several ejaculations, known as sexual satiety. It has been shown that androgen receptor expression is reduced after a single ejaculation, whether during sex or masturbating. The study also found that the relationship between increased orgasming, which leads to a decrease in androgen receptors in specific brain areas and reduced sexual motivation independently of testosterone levels.

Dopamine is at the core of our sexual drives and survival needs, and it motivates us to do just about everything. This mechanism within the reward center of the primitive brain has been around for millions of years and has not changed. Rats, humans, and indeed all mammals share this common mechanism for survival. Dopamine is behind a lot of the desire we associate with eating and sexual intercourse.

Similarly, all addictive drugs trigger dopamine and stimulate the pleasure/reward center. So do gambling, shopping, overeating, and other seemingly unrelated activities. Shopping, smoking, playing computer games, and orgasms are all associated with dopamine secretion. They all work somewhat differently on the brain, but all raise your dopamine levels. You get a bigger blast of dopamine eating high-calorie, high-fat foods than eating low-calorie vegetables. You don't really love pizza, cheeseburgers, or ice cream sundaes; rather, you really love that blast of dopamine that comes from it.

You're genetically programmed to seek out high-calorie foods over others. Similarly, dopamine drives you to have sex over most other activities. With dopamine as the driving force, nature has designed your biology to engage in sex (fertilization behavior to make more babies). Dopamine also urges men to move on to new partners to create greater genetic variety among their offspring.

The primitive male brain accomplishes these goals of more offspring and promiscuity by manipulating a man's brain chemistry and thus his desires and thoughts. High levels of dopamine increase a man's sexual desire, encouraging him to behave recklessly. It creates the thrill of a new affair and the rush from pornography. Unfortunately, consistently high levels of dopamine lead to erratic behavior and compulsions that are not good for a man's survival. That's why most mammals evolved with defined sexual periods when they "go into heat." The rest of the time, they are more or less neutral about sex.

Humans, however, don't have a period of "heat" followed by a long period of indifference to sex. Unlike other mammals, humans have the potential for ongoing, dopamine-driven sexual desire. Yet men self-regulate with an "off switch" that kicks in after they have too many orgasms. This drop in dopamine and rise in prolactin is the cause of the emotional separation that so often follows in the hours and even days after a man has sex and orgasms in a woman.

A balanced level of dopamine is necessary for good male mental health. When dopamine drops, men feel like something is wrong. Too much dopamine also leads to reckless behavior, which can be dangerous. A man then projects these uncomfortable feelings onto their female partner. Wow, a sexual hangover! Suddenly, she doesn't look so appealing. This is a very uncomfortable cycle to experience in your ongoing Female Led Relationship and damages a couple's intimacy.

During this sexual hangover (low dopamine) period in the relationship, the woman may feel abandoned while her man may feel like his woman is demanding sexual performance from him in a way that he simply cannot tolerate. This causes men and even women to desperately seek new highs like alcohol, sweets, new partners, pornography, and drugs. It is all merely an effort to raise your dopamine levels after the fall.

Perhaps men can now see how this cycle of highs and lows, or attraction and repulsion, can make their Female Led Relationship feel more like a roller coaster ride than the romantic fairytale I promised in *Love & Obey*. It is like starting to drive and then slamming on the brakes in heavy traffic, and it can make your FLR sick. It shows up in lovers' lives as intense attraction, followed by boredom and even disgust. Prolactin promotes a desire for separation from your partner as well. What's worse is that dopamine is not the only culprit contributing to the behaviors and mood swings that separate intimate partners emotionally.

Prolactin, the neurochemical that shoots up after orgasm, is associated with many of the biggest complaints that long-term couples (female led and even male led) experience in their relationships. Prolactin's effects can linger. If you ever tried cocaine, you will know what I mean. Cocaine blasts the brain with high levels of dopamine and makes you feel incredible, but during cocaine withdrawal, prolactin rises and brings you way down, so you want more cocaine. Indeed, addicts going through cocaine withdrawal require two weeks for their prolactin levels to drop to normal and dopamine levels to rise.

After mating, female rats show surges in prolactin for a week or two, even if they don't get pregnant. Prolactin is associated with stress because it makes you feel like life is hopeless. As men grow distressed and discouraged by the puzzling highs and lows in their relationships caused by their orgasms and changes in dopamine levels, their higher prolactin levels only compound their distress and relationship unhappiness. They forget what it feels like to be in balance and gradually lose their natural sense of wellbeing.

Both low dopamine and high prolactin levels make your world look dreary and increase your craving for more and better sex with new partners because your body naturally knows it will raise your dopamine levels. But, men, now you know that it will only set you on another sexually addictive cycle of highs and lows. Together, these neurochemicals create whatever the couple knows as the "end of the honeymoon." Most male led couples experience this fatigue within the first year of marriage.

CHAPTER 16

Why Do Women Love Chastity?

Why do women love Chastity? Women love male chastity because there is no greater sign of devotion as when a man hands over the control of his most precious power. When you place a cage on his penis, you signify that you essentially own him 100 percent. Male chastity can only work when the relationship is loving and strong, which is why a Female Led Relationship provides the perfect foundation.

A woman is finally given the opportunity to be in complete control and have a man who dutifully serves her. This is a gift because we only become better versions of ourselves when we have the support we need to grow and evolve. Your man in a supportive position offers his Queen the support she needs to do what she does best—lead the relationship. The idea that you can now take it a step further and control your man's penis is only a bonus, but it represents a very powerful step.

The first thing that happens is that every day he is in chastity ramps up the sexual focus and it can make this process extremely exciting. When the Queen is turned on and

94

eager to serve, this is likely to take intimacy and connectedness to a whole new level.

When a man gives up his "right" to ejaculate without his woman's permission and she allows him to have intercourse with her, both are stepping away from an old patriarchal conception of sex being performed for man's pleasure and that the man is independent. Once your man accepts male chastity, he is accepting a new sexual role. A role in which the woman is in control and the man submits and can relax because he does not have to pretend that he is in charge anymore.

As your Female Led Relationship evolves, ejaculation itself may be separated from the couple's increasingly female-focused sexuality. A man's "need" to ejaculate is vastly overrated and a clever wife can often train her husband to come on command, once a week or month, under her supervision. The rest of the time, if she desires his oral attentions and she enjoys penetration, his hard but obedient penis are all that is required for him to become your obedient sex slave. Once a man realizes that, he is no longer in charge of sexuality in your Female Led Relationship.

Once a man realizes that he is no longer even in charge of his ejaculations, he may be confused about his role, but trust me, he will also be relieved of performance anxiety.

Male chastity will also help him retain his semen and raise his testosterone levels and sexual energy, so even his performance will improve, and he will more than likely be very hard and more than eager to perform for his woman when she wants to fuck him. This all helps to create the female's lead role as the man becomes the subject of her attentions and enters the sub-zone where he is no longer obligated to initiate sex. In his new role, he will focus on how best to please his wife without thinking about his own pleasure because he will be aware that he's not allowed to orgasm while pleasuring his wife—except on rare occasions when she allows him his special treat.

While men may find this is frustrating at first, most men are simple creatures and will soon accept their wife's complete control of their sex life. Better still, because the now dominant wife only has sex when she wants it and how she wants it. As a result, the couple will tend to be a lot more sexually satisfied. The man will quickly learn that he is now in the role of serving his woman's desires, not his own.

Men, on average, take four minutes from the point of entry until ejaculation. Women usually take around ten to eleven minutes to reach orgasm. This means there is a real need for men to slow down and for women to control their ability to orgasm in favor of their men focusing on their pleasure. Men and women travel slightly different paths to arrive at sexual desire. Esther Perel, a New York City psychotherapist, says, "I hear women say in my office that desire originates much more between the ears than between the legs. "For women, there is a need for a plot—hence the romance novel. It is more about the anticipation, and how you get there; it is the longing that is the fuel for desire.

Women's desire "is more contextual, more subjective, more layered on a lattice of emotion," Perel adds. Perel also states that men, by contrast, don't need to have nearly as much imagination since sex is simpler and more straightforward for them. That doesn't mean men don't seek intimacy, love, and connection in a relationship, as women do. They just view the role of sex differently. "Women want to talk first, connect first, then have sex," Perel explains. "For men, sex is the connection. Sex is the language men use to express their tender loving vulnerable side," Perel says. "It is their language of intimacy."

Male chastity allows women to control the narrative and the lead-up to sex. By controlling their man's ability to orgasm and keep the focus on them, they can create many different ways to engage in romance, foreplay, and sex. It allows women to shape sex to suit their needs, which makes it more exciting for both. If the Queen is turned on, then her man is equally, if not more, motivated.

With female leadership in a relationship, the benefits don't stop at the bedroom door. A man who becomes sexually submissive to his woman will find that his sexuality and sense of masculinity will be transformed. He will become calmer and more at peace with himself. He will not have to be burdened with society's role of high sexual male expectations. He simply needs to do as he is told, and both he and his women will be happier than they've ever imagined possible. Male chastity will make men better lovers. Once a man orgasms, the sex is usually done. By the woman not allowing or delaying the male orgasm, she essentially trains him to focus on her pleasure longer. You, the Queen, can spend more time enjoying multiple orgasms.

One of the most desirable benefits of male chastity happens shortly after the lock is shut for the first time. Once your man gets his first restricted erection after being locked, sexual tension and frustration will rise up, and your sub-male will have a powerful desire to channel it somehow. Naturally, his thoughts will move toward his Key Holder. This growing sexual frustration will build, and the sub-male will find his Key Holder beyond irresistible. As the Key Holder, you will start receiving more frequent compliments, more affection, and love, and your sub-male will become more romantic. And he will have so much more gratitude when you interact with him in any way, especially sexually, even if it is only for your pleasure, like oral sex for you. Male chastity quickly creates your dream partner!

Another noticeable benefit is the higher couple's sex drive that naturally comes as a result of the greater intimacy. As the pent-up male frustration and tension continue to build, the more his behavior will be toward making you happy. Soon both of your positive feelings toward each other will begin to overflow, and the sex drive and libido will consume you both. Your man will want to pleasure you, the Key Holder as you have propelled into the number one spot in their mind.

Now instead of focusing on his own orgasm and masturbation, he is focused on everything he has to do to please his Queen. This is what every woman wants. It's the dream. The longer your man is locked, the more you will shape his behavior and the better he will become at serving you. When you demand oral sex to satisfy your needs first, the more practice he will get and the better he will be. All of a sudden, the bedroom will become so much more exciting and fulfilling.

Think of it as a female sexual guarantee that helps ensure your complete sexual satisfaction. Many men experienced premature ejaculation, and male chastity and orgasm control can train them to control their release. The Men's Clinic of UCLA says delayed ejaculation is the inability of a man to achieve climax within a reasonable amount of time. Some men cannot achieve ejaculations through vaginal penetration and must rely on alternative sexual acts to climax. Some men will lose their erection before achieving the climax and be left frustrated. Some men will reach the point of orgasm but can't finish and are left feeling very uncomfortable.

Delayed ejaculation is a neurological, hormonal, and psychological event. If a man has had damage to the nerves in his pelvis or had a spinal cord injury below the lower thoracic spinal level, he may suffer from an inability to ejaculate. He lacks the nerve connection from the ejaculation nerves at the tip of his penis back to his spinal cord. More commonly, he may have a hormonal imbalance in serotonin, prolactin, or testosterone. Men taking antidepressants, whose serotonin levels are skewed by the pills, frequently suffer from delayed or loss of ejaculation. Men with low testosterone also can have difficulty ejaculating.

So, if your man suffers from any of these conditions, chastity can divert his attention from the sex act to pleasuring the Queen or becoming aroused in other ways. Many men have reported feeling very aroused and fulfilled at the thought of just being under the Queen's control. Rather than place more stress on your man, male chastity allows him to relax and still enjoy sexual arousal and other forms of pleasure.

Lastly, masturbation can be a huge challenge for women. Many women are unhappy with the time their men spend masturbating. Men want sex more often than women at the start of a relationship, in the middle of it, and after many years of it. Men also say they want more sex partners in their lifetime and are more interested in casual sex. Men are more likely to seek sex even when it's frowned upon or even outlawed. About two-thirds say they masturbate, even though about half also say they feel guilty about it. By contrast, about 40 percent of women say they masturbate, and the frequency of masturbation is smaller among women.

The main purpose of sexuality is a union between two people who generally have some love and attraction for each other. The purpose of sexuality is abandoned in masturbation because the center of the sexual act becomes "me" instead of "we," and the person is trained to look to himself for sexual fulfillment. The gift of sexuality is misused for the sake of lifeless pleasure. When people misuse their sexuality in this way, they may begin to use pleasure to change their mood, release tension, or forget their loneliness.

Masturbation becomes an escape. It may pacify them, but it will never satisfy them. They use the fantasies of their mind and the pleasures of their body to flee from reality and the call to love. Their goal in sexual activity has been reduced to merely receiving pleasure instead of showing love. Women like chastity as a method to control their men masturbating. Chastity allows the Queen to control her man and the time he spends masturbating. In male chastity, a man's sexual energy should be reserved and focused on his woman.

CHAPTER 17

Why Do Men Love Chastity?

Why do men love male chastity? Why would he welcome having his penis locked up and engaged in male chastity? The answer may not be apparent at first. Most people new to Female Led Relationships or domination and submission may fail to understand the inner workings of chastity and find this practice to be abusive, barbaric, and downright inhumane. But just as all other practices that involve self-control and refraining from indulging in things, male chastity can lead to some very impressive and transformative results. As you have seen, at the physiological level, there are so many changes that occur.

If you ever had to go on a diet or give up drinking alcohol, the first few weeks were hell, but what happened long term? In terms of food, you lost weight and felt better, and in terms of alcohol, you felt clearer and healthier. Male chastity is similar. In many cultures, we have seen that the constant indulging in masturbation and ejaculation leads to depletion of life force. It's similar to fasting. Many cultures believe in a period of refraining from indulgence as a means of strengthening the body.

We have also seen how male chastity conducted in a loving relationship is transformative to men who later admit to becoming obsessed. Physically, a man feels better because his body is stronger and more energetic, and he builds willpower and even more desire for his woman. He can focus all of his attention on his Queen, which is really what he wanted all along.

What happens to men and women in male chastity is similar to what happens during dating. The man is fixated on the woman and desires sex with her, but the longer the fixation, the greater the desire. When you were dating, think of how many times you checked your phone, felt the excitement of seeing your man, and experienced little moments like the first kiss, holding hands, and the anticipation of sex. He was also 100 percent focused on you and your needs. These are just some examples that make dating so exciting.

Once you are in a marriage or relationship for years, there is no pursuit and less desire, and eventually, both of you are treating each other like an old shoe. You love your old shoe, and you would even be upset if you couldn't find your old shoe or it somehow disappeared, but it lost its novelty appeal. The anticipation, waiting, and desire for sex and togetherness are what exactly happens in male chastity when the Queen dictates when he should orgasm. Male chastity makes things new again because the woman now controls the power center of a man.

One of the fundamental aspects of social interaction is that some individuals have more influence than others. Social Power can be defined as the ability of a person to create conformity even when the people being influenced may attempt to resist those changes. Bosses have power over their workers, parents have power over their children, and, more generally, we can say that those in authority have power over their subordinates. In short, power refers to the process of social influence itself—those who have power are those most able to influence others.

Same is true when a woman has power over her man in a relationship or marriage. Men want a strong female figure in their lives so the idea of giving up the control and allowing their power centers to be controlled by a woman is very arousing. Once the Queen steps into her role as ultimate ruler and leader, the man will naturally take his position as the supporter. Ever need a man to make a grocery list on his own, then go get the groceries? He hates it. He is not interested in a leadership position in the household. Determine what he should get, give him a list, and he will gladly go do it. This is the supportive role and this is the role that men would prefer to be in.

Male chastity takes the role of supportive submissive to a whole new level. All of a sudden, men view their Queens in a much different light, which is why they get instantly aroused when she places all of her attention on him and locks up his cock and holds the key. It's a symbol of ultimate control. Men also feel more testosterone, become stronger, more invigorated, and excited. His focus will naturally be on his Queen, and wearing the cage reminds him of whom he owes his allegiance.

In previous books, I have discussed the idea that men always need and respond to a leader. Without proper leadership, they feel chaotic with no direction and purpose. In the study Sex-Role Obedience to Authority by Geffner and Gross, obedience by male and female subjects to male and female experimenters was investigated. The four main factorial independent variables were the sex of the experimenter, the sex of the subject, and two conditions of presence or absence of a uniform presence or absence of an explanation. The results revealed there was more obedience with a uniform and more disobedience by females, which suggests that men are more likely to obey an authority figure.

Men need a purpose and a goal, so male chastity helps them to focus that purpose where it should be in all relationships—on the Queen. Think about it—are you happier in a good, fulfilling deep relationship or a bad relationship with arguments and daily power struggles? With male chastity, there is no argument, and men can do what they do best—be the supportive gentleman. This goes to the foundation of the female led lifestyle, which is why Female Led Relationships are so successful. Men love male chastity because each day is new and unpredictable, and their Queen is focused on sex every day. When you are controlling his penis, you are in ultimate control over everyone else in his life. When he wears a cock cage, he will be thinking of you all day long.

Going back to the research on men and authority—men respond much better when there is a firm authority figure in their lives. When they are younger, this person is their mother, and maybe their father. For at least 50 percent of the men out there, with a divorce at 50 percent, men live and answer to a female figure, and it is believed that they crave this in a partner. The Queen replaces the mother as the authority figure, which is why Female Led Relationships are in demand. It's a win-win situation for you and your man because he will respond to your instruction, and you can be in charge.

CHAPTER 18

Tantric Sex and Chastity

Tantric sex is powerful in chastity to allow you and your Queen to delay orgasm and enjoy prolonging the whole experience. The three major keys to moving energy in Tantra are breath, sound, and movement. Using these three keys, you can practice "running" your sexual energy throughout your body, whether you're engaged in sensual play or alone, and you can amp it up until it spills over into an energetic orgasm. It can be such a profound and empowering aspect of connecting with your own innate sensuality. Steps to begin to get into the Tantric sex mood include getting prepared and creating the kind of space you'd like to be in to have any other kind of orgasm.

Foreplay can be anything you want it to be—oral, a massage, taking a shower together. But whatever you do, make sure you and your partner are fully present. Sit in front of your man. Look into each other's eyes. Start to move your bodies slightly as you breathe. After five minutes, start to touch each other sensually, taking turns massaging each other's arms, legs, neck, and other parts. After another five minutes, begin to kiss—and only kiss. Focus on every physical sensation you're feeling in the moment.

You both need to go within. Turn your attention inward, closing your eyes to signal to the mind that it's time to relax and let go. Open up the breath. Take some long, deep breaths to start, relaxing your entire body. Let the breath melt through any tension anywhere inside you. Then move into circular breathing, with no pause between exhaling or inhaling. Connect to your sensuality. Focus your attention at the level of the genitals; connect to the quality of pleasure and eroticism within you. Fantasizing and caressing the whole body can help get you in the mood. Massage is vital to tantric sex, but not just any massage. Schedule a block of time and take the time to explore your man's body and vice versa.

The Yoni massage is a tantric massage technique designed to allow the Queen to relax and receive pleasure. *Yoni* is a Sanskrit word for the vagina, meaning "Sacred Space," and the vagina is viewed with the utmost love and respect. Yoni massage focuses on pleasure for the vagina, while the Queen can focus on all the sensual pleasure. While your man is in chastity, he can focus on giving you a Yoni massage as an alternative to intercourse. Tantric sex is great for male chastity because it involves delayed or controlled orgasms, but Tantra involves much more than just orgasms. Holding off on orgasm relates to the concept of channeling sexual energy through the body instead of releasing it through climax. Tantric couples often tout the benefits of retaining this energy as far as increased physical power and stamina—many will tell you that it feels incredible.

The goal of Tantra is to remain mindful of every sensation during the encounter, both in the context of giving and receiving. By staying mindful and basking in the experience itself, you build intense energy and affinity for your partner. This is where intimacy is created and where the bonding takes place. Harnessing sexual energy is thought by many to be vital to our physical health. Sex can help regulate the stress response and increase serotonin levels. By giving and receiving during sex, you're not only giving your partner pleasure, but you're also giving the gift of health. Nothing could be deeper or more soothing than this level of care.

Benefits of Tantra

Here are all the benefits of Tantra that you and your man can experience:

- Awakening your sexual energy to flow freely within your body.

- Accessing your fullest pleasure and desire.

- Tuning into subtle energy.

- Discovering full-body and/or multiple orgasms.

- Experiencing a new level of heart connection with your partner's profound sense of intimacy and loving presence.

- Longer lovemaking sessions, relaxation, and quality of spaciousness.

- Enhanced communication and communion.

- Holistic mind-body-spirit connection with yourself and with your partner.

CHAPTER 19

Attachment Styles and Female Led Relationships

Relationships are affected by several factors, and attachment styles can have an impact on the success of your relationship. Attachment is the bond we form with our first primary caregiver, usually a parent, and the way we develop it eventually affects the way we find, keep, and end relationships. In *Psychology Today*, based on research by Bartholomew and Horowitz, there are four adult attachment styles: Secure, Anxious-Preoccupied, Dismissive-Avoidant, and Fearful-Avoidant. Depending on which category you and your Queen fall into, this can affect your Female Led Relationship success. The following are the four attachment styles and traits that tend to be associated with each.

Secure Attachment Style

- Higher emotional intelligence. Capable of conveying emotions appropriately and constructively.

- Capable of sending and receiving healthy expressions of intimacy.

- Capable of drawing healthy, appropriate, and reasonable boundaries when required.

- Feel secure being alone as well as with a companion.

- Tend to have a positive view of relationships and personal interactions.

- More likely to handle interpersonal difficulties in stride. Discuss issues to solve problems rather than to attack a person.

- Resiliency in the face of relational dissolution. Capable of grieving, learning, and moving on.

Anxious-Preoccupied Attachment Style

- Inclined to feel more nervous and less secure about relationships in general and romantic relationships in particular.

- Inclined to have many stressors in relationships based on both real and imagined happenings. These stressors can manifest themselves through a variety of possible issues such as neediness, possessiveness, jealousy, control, mood swings, oversensitivity, obsessiveness, etc.

- Reluctant to give people the benefit of the doubt, a tendency for automatic negative thinking when interpreting others' intentions, words, and actions.

- Requires constant stroking of love and validation to feel secure and accepted. Responds negatively when not provided with regular positive reinforcement.

- Drama oriented. Constantly working on (sometimes inventing) relationship issues in order to seek validation, reassurance, and acceptance. Some feel more comfortable with stormy relationships than calm and peaceful ones.

- Dislike being without company. Struggle being by oneself.

- History of emotionally turbulent relationships.

Dismissive-Avoidant Attachment Style

- Highly self-directed and self-sufficient. Independent behaviorally and emotionally.

- Avoid true intimacy, which makes one vulnerable, and may subject the Dismissive-Avoidant to emotional obligations.

- Desire freedom physically and emotionally ("No one puts a collar on me." Pushes away those who get too close ("I need room to breathe.")

- Other priorities in life often supersede a romantic relationship, such as work, social life, personal projects and passions, travel, fun, etc. In these situations, the partner is frequently excluded or holds only a marginal presence.

- Many have commitment issues. Some prefer to be single than to settle down. Even in committed relationships, they prize autonomy above much else.

- May have many acquaintances but few truly close relationships.

Fearful-Avoidant Attachment Style

- Often associated with highly challenging life experiences such as grief, abandonment, and abuse.

- Desire but simultaneously resist intimacy. Much inner conflict.

- Struggle with having confidence in and relying on others.

- Fear annihilation, physically and/or emotionally in loving, intimate situations.

- Similar to the Anxious-Preoccupied Style, suspicious of others' intentions, words, and actions.

- Similar to the Dismissive-Avoidant Style, pushes people away and has few genuinely close relationships.

Those who are predominantly the Secure Attachment Style tend to make strong partners, but other attachment styles can also make great relationships. This type finds it easy to be close to others and is comfortable depending on others—they don't mind being depended on. They rarely worry about being abandoned or someone getting too close to them. They have a positive self-view and perceive others positively. These beliefs give them the capacity to ask for what they want in a relationship or ask for clarity. They don't feel they have to manipulate or convince someone they are good enough.

Challenges can occur when certain types are attracted to each other and do not often form successful unions. Anxious and Avoidant Attachment Styles are often attracted to each other and make up about half of the total population. Opposites do attract but also reaffirms the other's beliefs about themselves and relationships. The avoidant's belief that others will want more closeness than they are comfortable with will be confirmed. The anxious ones who believe they want more intimacy than their partner can provide will also be confirmed.

The Anxious Avoidant trap is where the anxious one is preoccupied with intimacy and the avoidant one wants to avoid it. Even when they love each other very much, they can easily get trapped in a cycle of exacerbating each other's insecurities. Their colliding intimacy needs often result in a stormy relationship that can be destructive. Researchers suggested that what happens is a combination of misreading by one partner and a fair amount of strategizing by the insecure partner. They point out that anxiously attached people may seem fascinating at first, and their preoccupation may easily be confused with self-disclosure and openness, which facilitates a sense of connection.

Similarly, an avoidant person may come across as independent and strong. In a series of experiments, the team discovered that avoidants—even though they don't want emotional connection—made lots of eye contact and used touch more than securely attached people to appear more appealing in a dating situation. Avoidants appear to use humor in dating situations to create a sense of sharing and detract from their essential aloofness. People with insecure attachment styles of anxious or avoidant tend not to approach conflict head-on. Anxious/avoidant couples often struggle to find solutions acceptable to both of them.

Conflict is sometimes left unresolved because the resolution itself would create too much intimacy for the avoidant partner. Conflicts then repeat. In these clashes, the anxious partner is more often the one who loses ground. People with Insecure Attachment Styles also don't communicate as effectively as securely attached individuals in intimate relationships.

Studies on patterns of human attachment and whether people got anxious when they were in romantic relationships revealed that being romantically attached gives rise to anxiety for multiple reasons, ranging from the fear of revelations about themselves to the fear of losing the person with whom they are in love. For others, rather than face this anxiety, they become avoidant. Avoiding the feelings associated with romance helps people cope with it. Yet, both of these ways of attaching, although very common, prevent deeper intimacy. Do men and women differ with regard to romantic attachment?

Overall, men tended to be more avoidant and less anxious than women. When men are attached, rather than dealing with the many anxieties involved in romance, they distanced themselves from them. In effect, they avoided the feelings and the romantic attachment. Women, on the other hand, were more prone to being anxious. Being attached made them feel more anxiety and the closeness was emotionally disruptive. The problem with this is that both of these results make you want to leave the relationship rather than dive in deeper. It also causes arguments. Women may become resentful that men are "clueless" or not feeling the anxiety that they are feeling. Men become resentful that women are too "high-strung" about simple issues. And it does not necessarily help if men become anxious or women become avoidant to be more like their partners. The problem of never being truly intimate still exists.

We may not be able to control the attachment styles and bonds we form, but we can help to prevent issues in a Female Led Relationship with more communication and establishing of trust. In an FLR, there is likely to be more discussion about the marriage or relationship, so more opportunity to identify and solve problems as they happen. Women tend to need more intimacy and a feeling of connection so by having her man's complete attention she is more likely to feel secure if she is more inclined to have an anxious attachment style. Men tend to be more avoidant so by having your Queen's attention daily and allowing her to take charge, you are less likely to fall into patterns of distancing, withdrawing and being more aloof.

Chapter 20

Cuckolding and the Female Led Relationship

C uckolding and the Female Led Relationship is becoming more popular, and it's becoming one of the most fascinating sexual activities in relationships. There is growing interest in Cuckolding from both men and women, even though it is not mandatory to engage in cuckolding as part of a Female Led Relationship. A cuckold is someone who takes pleasure in watching their partner have sex with someone else. There have been many ways in which cuckolding is executed in a relationship, and historically, it was frowned upon since the man would be ridiculed for the assumption that he was unable to perform during sex, leading his partner to seek out another man to satisfy her.

Today, however, cuckolding is much more complex, and this is due to women taking the lead and making the decisions in relationships. Cuckolding is much more than just having sex with another person and requires establishing many rules for everything to go smoothly. I was once a critic of cuckolding since I believed engaging with a third person and introducing them into the relationship would surely cause a rift that would have disastrous consequences. Cuckolding also goes against monogamy, which has been the gold standard for relationships. But at 150,000 searches a month on Google in North America alone, it is growing in popularity.

After investigating the habits of many couples already involved in this lifestyle, I have come to appreciate the reasons why people are obsessed with it. I also have a much deeper understanding of how cuckolding can transform a relationship. Even researchers agree—according to their research, cuckolding couples who act on their desires feel liberated because they can be honest about their sexual fantasies, which leads to more open communication than couples in "normal" relationships. Couples feel closer because there is no hiding or sneaking around.

Today, relationships are dramatically different than they were 20 years ago. The divorce rate is still around 50 percent and infidelity, lying, and dishonesty play a huge role in the destruction of many relationships. But what if this could all change?

What if we could be open to our partner's desires and make their happiness our main priority? What if couples could feel completely at ease discussing their needs and wants openly without judgement? Could there be fewer arguments and sneaking around? Could there be more intimacy and sharing, rather than jealousy? I have witnessed couples who have reported a complete turnaround in their relationship when open, honest communication and a willingness to try new things are implemented.

In all industries, change is daunting. What if we never accepted home computers or mobile phones? What if we still needed to talk on the phone instead of texting and there was no social media, just in person social gatherings? How would our lives be different? The same is true for cuckolding. What was once a major taboo is becoming much more mainstream, and as controversial as it is, cuckolding is here to stay. The only question will be—how does it work in your relationship? This book will provide a guide for cuckolding and the rules, which you will need to follow to be successful. I will also cover how to start cuckolding and how to avoid the common pitfalls. This book will also offer the female perspective since, generally, she is in charge and makes the decision of what is right for her and her man.

Maybe you are a woman who is interested in adding cuckolding to your current sexual activities? How do you reassure your man and execute it successfully? Maybe you are a man who wants your wife or girlfriend to engage in cuckolding. How do you introduce it?

Today, more than 50 percent of couples have a cheating spouse and many end in divorce, so the old ways are not working. Blame new lifestyles, a society that wants instant pleasure, or a change in values. But something has to change. Cuckolding could be an answer to some of the issues leading to infidelity, and there seems to be less lying, deceit, and dishonesty by their lovers and life partners, whether married or in a committed relationship. A relationship that is exciting, loving, honest, and filled with trust should be the new standard.

For me, trust is the most important, rarest and difficult quality to maintain in a long-term relationship, especially one that involves sex with more than one person. No matter the controversy, cuckolding is here to stay. This book offers a guide on how to engage in it while maintaining a strong bond with your Queen. It is my hope that both men and women will gain tremendous insight into this world, which can lead to safe and happy exploration. This should be an adventure that you do together with consent from all parties involved.

In the media, cuckolding has become mainstream. In the Emmy nominated show *Succession* on Netflix, Shiv Roy has her husband sign a contract mutually agreeing she will be having sex with other men. Today, more millennials have admitted to engaging in cuckolding on a regular basis with no issues in the main relationship, and dozens of sites are dedicated to it. Wealthy couples often used cuckolding in which the man was much older than his woman and got to the age when he was unable to perform. In these types of relationships, men often participate in finding their wife's Bull and will watch their sex act.

In my last three books *Love & Obey, Real Men Worship Women,* and *Oral Sex for Women,* I focus on the Female Led Relationship where cuckolding is the decision of the woman. She makes the ultimate rule of whether she wants to engage in cuckolding and the man agrees. Even traditionally, cuckolding was initiated by the woman, so I feel that it is mainly a female-dominated realm. This book will focus on cuckolding from the female perspective. However, if you are a man who wants to introduce it to your Queen, this will also help her to get excited since it is a female-driven activity with supportive participation.

In Female Led Relationships, the man's responsibility—under his submission to the female's absolute authority over him—is to allow her freedom, so she can achieve happiness and as much pleasure as possible in her life. Cuckolding, in my opinion, should be approached in a similar manner to the *Love & Obey* philosophy in which the woman is the Queen and her man is the supportive gentleman making all of her fantasies, including cuckolding, come true. Why is this so important? Because a woman's happiness in a relationship is mandatory. No man can ever exist in a happy relationship without his Goddess also being happy. I have had my share of critics' attempts to argue that my writings are solely for female's control over men; however, the saying, "happy wife, happy life" is true for this very reason.

Whether you are in a Female Led Relationship or not, when the Queen is unhappy, it makes for a very rocky and unsuccessful relationship. FLR cuckolding is the modern style of cuckolding, as the Queen exercises control over her own body, her autonomy from patriarchal and primary male possession, misogynist control, slut-shaming, criticism, and her absolute right to act freely on her emotional and sexual desires as a strong, independent, and powerful woman.

Let's face it, women are leading in so many ways and exercising their authority more than ever. In 80 percent of the couples I have interviewed, the men agree that they will follow the lead of their women even though it was not formally established that they are in a Female Led Relationship. So, in general, many men welcome the idea of spicing up their relationship with the introduction of a Bull, and they can still participate by watching or being included, depending on the direction of their woman.

For some men, they are turned on by the fantasy of seeing their wife or girlfriend with a man who is more well-endowed or of a different race. In this case, he has to convince his Queen to engage in this type of activity, and it is so much simpler if the woman feels she is in control of the situation. Sometimes cuckolding is used as a form of humiliation—for being the pathetic slave who cannot satisfy his Goddess and must sit quietly why another man satisfies her. So, there are many variations and ways cuckolding can be executed with absolute consent from all three parties.

Relationships can be challenging, and there are so many cases recently in which couples are looking for ways to spice up the relationship. We all like variety. As women, we love wearing different outfits, shoes, and bags. Men love driving different cars and going to various bars. Some people love being around people of different nationalities or trying different foods—people want variety, and I believe that they need it in their relationships.

As the leader of the female led movement, which was originally frowned upon, I have noticed how receptive people are to this change in power. Men are requesting it, and women are loving it. Many couples are changing the dynamic in relationships because they are looking for variety and ways to fulfill an inner need. There are very few relationships that break up over cuckolding. But 50 percent of traditional marriages still end in divorce. It's a fact that fewer couples in Female Led Relationships divorce. This suggests that even though this is a radical movement, there is something about it that actually bonds couples.

Research shows that 4 to 5 percent of heterosexual couples have agreed to have an open relationship. In other words, they've given their consent not to be monogamous. The National Opinion Research Center's General Social Survey revealed that more than 20 percent of married men and nearly 15 percent of married women admit to infidelity, a number that's risen almost 40 percent for women in the past 20 years.

In addition, some studies have found that between 30 and 60 percent of married individuals in the United States will engage in adultery at some point in their marriage. So, while only 4 to 5 percent of men and women are choosing to be open about their extramarital relations, somewhere between 15 and 60 percent are opting for a less consensual form of infidelity. Cuckolding is not infidelity, and in general, it is done together with consent.

CHAPTER 21

Why Does Cuckolding Change Relationships?

C uckolding is transforming relationships, and increased depiction in mainstream media coupled with millions of searches a month online confirms this finding. Research and psychologists have found that when a man or woman sees their partner with someone else, it can excite them and give them feelings of being proud to be with someone who is desired by others. Men and women with attractive partners get this feeling when people are paying lots of attention to their husbands, wives, girlfriends, or boyfriends. Sometimes we all feel good when others want what we have. It's a basic human emotion.

As an extension, realizing your inability to satisfy your partner sexually and be okay with someone else doing it is also exciting and builds a feeling of trust and control because it is condoned by the partner getting cucked. Couples often race home to tell their stories and share the experience openly. Some individuals like the humiliation and feeling of subservience. This is true in some Female Led Relationships in which men will be happy when their Goddess, who they serve, is allowed to choose any man she wants. They get turned on by the humiliation they feel when a stronger and more virile man is satisfying his Queen sexually.

Humiliation seems to play a leading role in cuckolding. For some, humiliation ramps up the erotic intensity. Most men are turned on and enjoy watching their partner with someone else. They even love it when their woman laughs or belittles the Bull she's with. Pleasure also comes from this being the ultimate show of respect to allow your woman to do what she wants.

CHAPTER 22

Cuckolding and Humiliation

C uckolding becomes a significant part of a Female Led Relationship because some men enjoy being subservient and also like the humiliation aspect of the lifestyle. They are turned on by humiliation. Many people relish consensual degradation, and in an FLR, some men find themselves serving their wife and her lover drinks or maybe cleaning the house in the buff while their woman reads on the couch. For these men, the line between eroticism and embarrassment is deeply rewarding.

It's also worth mentioning that humiliation and shame are cousins of guilt. Although there are deep chasms separating these emotions from one another, guilt absolutely plays a role in why some men want a Female Led Relationship. These days, many men are overwhelmed by the benefits they receive every day from male privilege. For a lot of them, the tremendous ease with which they wade through the world contrasts harshly against the ways they know their wife or girlfriend is treated daily by the outside world.

A Female Led Relationship helps them, in some ways, flip the script and reject the notions that have been pushed on them for their entire lives. Often, but not always, Female Led Relationships have strong ties to cuckold culture. The world of cuckolding is bursting with nuance, but a common thread through all styles of cucking is female dominance. The woman in the relationship controls sex, and often has sex with other men.

Depending on the agreement she and her partner reached, she either sleeps with the other men while her husband stays home and cleans. Or she lets her partner watch her get it on with another person. Sometimes, cuckold relationships even entail the man helping the woman pick out her new partners, and he may help her get ready for a date. Drawing her bath, getting her outfit ready, doing her hair, and painting her nails are all common tasks a woman may require of her partner.

Of course, you can have a Female Led Relationship that doesn't involve cuckolding too. Not all people who explore this dynamic feel called to engage in non-monogamy, too. In some situations, a Female Led Relationship simply means the woman is in charge. This still rears its head in the sack in a few different ways. For instance, she may be in charge of initiating sex—either by scheduling it or being the one who decides when it'll happen.

Other reasons for couples wanting cuckolding are to gain excitement from the forbidden. I grew up a very devout Catholic. So much so that I was afraid to steal a pack of gum, much less engage in sex with another man while my partner watched. In my early relationships, I could recall flying into a rage if my boyfriend's eye moved to look at another woman. This jealousy and rigid behavior caused me to become very angry and always worried about cheating.

One of my initial boyfriends suggested an open relationship, and I can recall being so upset about it that I secretly knew we were over. Once I broke out of these restraints based on religious conditioning, I was free to enjoy my relationships. I became less judgmental and more experimental, and I have never regretted a day of delving into this world. It changed my life, my relationship, and my outlook.

Relationships are one of the biggest influences in our lives, which can be a curse every day or a new opportunity to explore and gain more enjoyment and happiness. Once you push those boundaries, you are set free. So, while cuckolding is new, it's growing. I never thought Ashley Madison would become such a large organization spread across hundreds of countries. I realized that there were millions of people searching for new types of relationships. As much as I criticized infidelity, I was open to understanding the trends and changes happening in relationships.

CHAPTER 23

Set Rules and Boundaries for Cuckolding

Couples engaging in Cuckolding must have rules and boundaries which clearly define what occurs in the relationship, and these must be extended to include the Bull. One of the first rules to establish is where cuckolding will happen. Will it be at your house or the Bull's? Since your comfort is important and safety is mandatory, having it in an environment you all can handle is best. Some couples may choose a hotel room for complete anonymity, which is not a bad choice. You can reserve it and invite the Bull over. Everyone is safe and you are not entering private space.

If this is not an option, you can choose your guest bedroom, ensuring kids are not around. This way it's, again, not in your private space. You can also choose your pool area, if the weather permits, as it's sexy and again allows you to keep your personal areas private. The idea is that since this is a new adventure, keeping it separate from your day-to-day life is recommended.

When you have decided to do cuckolding, it is important to set up clearly defined boundaries with you and your Queen first. How will it play out? Will your Queen approach the Bull, or will both of you? Will the Queen decide how it will play out by giving you instructions, or will you be participating right from the start? This is where a Female Led Relationship is so beneficial because the woman makes the rules.

She decides on what will happen, and all you need to do is follow. So, boundaries must also involve what happens if anyone becomes uncomfortable or wants to stop. It should be clearly established that you will all abort immediately. Getting into arguments of jealous fits of rage should never occur. This keeps everything running smoothly. Maybe your Queen wants to stop. The appropriate and respectful response is to all agree. The Bull's state of mind must also be considered, and if he is unable to perform, you decide a respectful way to stop. At no time should anyone be made to feel pathetic or bad. You want to prevent any chance of a fun situation spiraling out of control.

Another important point in boundaries is to discuss the importance of honesty. The bond between you and your woman must be maintained, and at no time should either of you engage with the Bull alone or without consent. The idea of cuckolding as opposed to cheating is the lying, hiding, and secrecy that often occurs with infidelity. Maintaining trust is the biggest factor. I noticed that often in cheating it is the dishonesty that does the most destruction to relationships, which is why trust and the understanding that both people will always be honest and open about cuckolding is the key. It should be understood that there will be no emotional ties with the Bull from either of you.

These are some of the steps to begin:

The best place to start is with open communication. Discuss everything very openly. What do you like, and what does she like? How do you see the activity unfolding? What things are completely forbidden? Which areas would you be open to exploring?

The next step is to spend some time talking about the fantasy, so you can explore anything uncomfortable about it. Communication about everything is going to make things so much smoother. Decide on safe words to say if there is anything that feels strange and alarming.

Then, it's time to go out and engage with people. Just spend some time talking about it or hanging out with others in a bar setting. Without directly engaging a single man, you could set up scenarios to approach a single man in a bar with the goal of merely gaining experience of both of you being comfortable talking with a third. Maybe your Queen wants to dance with another man and flirt with him while you watch. This can be an easy way to determine how you and she feels about it.

One of my first experiences with this was when one of my ex-boyfriends encouraged me to dance with a friend of his. At first, I was a bit shocked that he did not care, and I was extremely uncomfortable with the other man being aggressive coming onto me in front of my boyfriend who had no issue with it. I later learned that it was something he liked and he and his friend were used to it. Needless to say, the relationship ended, but what I learned was that dancing and flirting in a scenario like this was enough to determine if cuckolding will be right for you.

If you both cannot get past this step or there are signs of jealousy, you may not be ready. It is important to get comfortable with the process and feel okay if the first time does not go well. After each encounter, even at a bar, discuss your feelings about it openly. Discuss any hesitations and how it could be improved. Maybe you did not like how she positioned herself with a third and excluded you. Or you like that she took the initiative to approach a man, then inviting both of you to sit and chat. It is imperative to discuss everything and ultimately decide if it is worth pursuing. I can recall one of my ex-boyfriends asking me to be in an open relationship and I said that I was fine with it, but in reality, I was not ready to pursue anything at the time. I think it was my unwillingness to be honest that eventually drove a rift between us.

The next step is to go online. Lots of dating sites are already set up for cuckolding, with many mainstream ones providing options to explore this. Spend time reading and looking at profiles and deciding together who would be suitable to join you both. Be respectful when you first approach someone and, again, make the first dates a time to just meet and talk. The more comfortable you are with the Bull—the better it will be. Keep personal details to a minimum and make sure everyone is onboard with safety and precautions.

Make some general rules for the night. For example, you may say to your partner: "Tonight, let's go out with Dan to dinner, and afterwards we can come back, go in the hot tub, and just start there." Nothing has to happen. It can just be a night of getting to know him and having fun. Later on, as you get more comfortable, you can have some hot times in a hot tub with kissing or allowing the Bull to feel her up. The Queen's decision about how far she is willing to go must be established, but there is no harm in starting with baby steps. The more smoothly each encounter goes, the better it is. Some couples progress with fingering or use of sex toys only as the exploration continues. Then once everyone is on board, you can all plan for the full experience of the Bull having intercourse with your woman while you watch.

Some variations can be that perhaps before intercourse, you can have oral sex with your woman, then let her be fucked by the Bull. Whatever happens, she must make the rules, and you can decide if you agree. It's much more fun and inclusive for you to participate in some way, with the main act to be reserved for the woman with the Bull.

Do not feel ashamed if you are feeling jealousy. Jealousy is a powerful human emotion. It doesn't mean you're closed-minded or prudish. No matter how "cool" you are, jealousy is going to flare up. That doesn't mean that "this kind of relationship isn't for you." Jealousy typically means you need some special attention. As a partner in a significant relationship with someone, you must be willing to work through feelings. Opening yourselves up to new sexual experiences can bring on all sorts of feelings, and you must be allowed to experience them openly. Many couples go through this, and it is perfectly normal. The emotions are part of the thrill ride, the jealousy, the passion, and the desire all wrapped up in your feelings, which is what makes this so exciting to everyone involved. You both also need to be respectful of the Bull and of any hesitations.

Humans seem to have evolved to be primarily monogamous, with occasional cheating, said University of Michigan psychology professor William McKibbin, PhD. As a result, about 4 percent of children worldwide are fathered by someone other than the man who believes he is the father, according to a meta-analysis published in the *Journal of Epidemiological Community Health* (Vol. 59, No. 9). That tendency allows females to have more genetic variation among their offspring, but for the cuckolded man, not good.

To defend against cuckoldry, men have developed a variety of behavioral and biological defenses, McKibbin said. He also found   that men at greater risk for cuckoldry, as measured by the proportion of time they'd spent away from their partners, became more interested in having sex with their partners.

They also found their partners more attractive and engaged in "mate guarding" behavior. This effect was independent of the amount of time since the couple last had sex, so it wasn't just the result of built-up desire—and it was moderated by how much a man trusted his mate not to cheat, McKibbin found. One such finding, in McKibbin's *Comparative Psychology* study, indicates: Men at risk for cuckoldry were later more likely to pressure their partners into having sex. More sex in this case is not always better because it is driven by fear. In this case, the trust factor is also threatened, which could lead to long-term issues.

The First Cuckolding Encounter

Now that all of the discussion, practice, and agreement has happened, it's now time to get to your first encounter. This is likely to have lots of excitement and anticipation. Ensure you are equipped with your safety items: condoms, birth control, etc. You may want to have a set of sheets set aside specifically for this. Even better, if it happens in a hotel room or a place that is apart from your main home. If you have kids, ensure you do not expose them in any way to this activity.

I recommend setting schedules and choosing a time to meet. It may be a good idea to meet at a restaurant or bar. You should both try to dress to impress in something applicable to the act. If your Queen wants to have extra outfits or sex toys, she can pack these things. Personal hygiene is of the utmost importance, which is why a hotel room works so that you have access to a bathroom. If you decide to have it in your home, it might be wise to designate a specific room for it so you can set it up, with mood and ambiance of your choosing. Pools, hot tubs, Jacuzzis, beachfront with access to a beach, or a penthouse suite overlooking the city are all wonderful areas to reserve for the first encounter.

When you first get to the place, start with getting everyone comfortable. Have some drinks and listen to music. You can begin with some light play with your Queen. Just engage slowly and sexy to get everyone in the mood. Then you can all move to the bedroom. If you Queen has decided you will watch, go to your chair and allow her to lead.

She should already have determined how she wants to have intercourse and allow things to unfold naturally. Be open and stick to your established boundaries. No one should go off-script.

It may be wise to make the first encounter short. Be aware of how you feel during the first time, so you can decide if cuckolding will happen again in the future. The key is to enjoy the moment. Focus on your Queen and her enjoyment. Refrain from intervening unless she specifically allows you to jump in. Then, only focus your attention on her. The more comfortable you all get, the better things will flow. Once you are done, the Bull can leave, and you both can continue together, cuddle or talk. Take showers or just unwind. It is essential to have a period of togetherness after the act.

CHAPTER 24

Hot-Wifing

C uckolding and hotwifing are similar ways of expressing your sexuality as a couple while allowing your wife to have a good time. The main difference between cuckolding and hotwifing involves the man who prefers to watch his wife with a man who is more well-endowed and can satisfy his woman better. A cuckold is usually a man who enjoys being humiliated for being inadequate. He has a smaller penis and is unable to satisfy his woman. He may simply enjoy seeing another man with his woman. Hotwifing is when men get enjoyment from showing off their women and the reaction of other men, but he still prefers to be alpha in the relationship or marriage.

In cuckolding, sometimes the dominant woman insists that she wants to have sex with a Bull, so it's much more of a female led activity. Hotwifing is much more male led because the husband derives pleasure from other men enjoying his wife. He may even be adequate and get involved in the sex act with the other man. A hotwifing husband considers it a compliment to himself that other men desire his wife. He takes pride in having such a hot wife who is sexually charged.

Cuckolding and hotwifing experiences are similar—a married woman engages in sexual relationships with other men with her man's consent. Often, these relationships are in pursuit of fulfilling the husband's or the couple's fantasies, and this can apply to any woman whose husband feels she is hot enough to attract another man or for the cuckold in which he is not sexually capable of solely satisfying her. In the world of kinky sex, either form of expression simply means the husband desires some level of interaction between his wife and another man.

While the concept of another man holding, kissing, and making love to your wife is typically considered to be a bit abnormal, it is a fantasy that many men and women have. In fact, research has shown that a majority of men fantasize about watching their wife engage in some degree of sexual activity with another man. Today, many couples consider cuckolding or hotwifing to be fun, exciting, and beneficial to their marriage. It is obvious why women like it since it allows them to fulfill their wildest sexual fantasies. In addition, many couples share this sexual fantasy of taking their relationship to a kinkier level.

Research shows that couples have fantasies about hotwifing, but many are afraid to express themselves because they fear what their partner might think of them. So, one of the benefits of acting on a hotwifing fantasy is the real-life fulfillment of your most secret desire. It also provides women with a newfound modern freedom and the right for her to choose what she does with her body. Modern women do not want to be controlled by a man.

In female led marriage, women have the right to do as they see fit. The wife gets the freedom to enjoy the company of the opposite sex. Many women in female led marriages enjoy the company of men other than their husbands. They practice the idea that modern women are "not the property of their husbands." This modern way is allowing women to have the chance to enjoy life more. When a man allows his woman to be in the company of other men, she enjoys a refreshing kind of intimacy and freedom with all her men, including her husband.

In female led marriage, women are freed from the jealousy of their husbands. Jealousy is one of the major reasons many relationships fail. Jealousy arises from male ego concerns and male insecurities. This male ego-based jealousy is a contributing factor in many disagreements and breakups. As we learned, jealousy comes from ancient genetic coding in men to protect their future lineage by making sure that his wife's offspring are his as well. Hotwifing is a modern experience involving birth control, which can help to rid the man of his feelings of jealousy. In a female led marriage, the wife can enjoy her freedom to be who she wants to be. She knows her husband will be obedient, and he will have her best interests and her pleasure at heart, which helps her trust him more and enjoy the marriage.

Relationships are built on trust and communication. Hotwifing can increase trust and communication within relationships. If you want to be truly happy, with a lasting relationship, you must ensure that you understand each other and also give one another the chance and freedom to be who you really are, including living out your most secret fantasies. Before you begin to dive into actual hotwifing or cuckolding, you both need to agree with each other of your intent to participate. The women in Female Led Relationships are typically sexually dominant, while the man takes on a more submissive role, only becoming involved with her sexually or with her lover when the wife permits him to. Sometimes the man will remain in chastity and completely celibate for the entire marriage.

As a man, you may feel that you are with the hottest woman on earth, and it's every man's desire to have a woman who is another man's dream. Hotwifing gives a man the perfect chance to allow other men to appreciate how beautiful and desirable his woman is, which typically serves to increase both his love and respect for her. It boosts both the man and the woman's confidence. In female led marriages and both cuckolding and hotwifing experiences, women have a chance to express themselves. When a woman knows that she has the support of her man to do whatever she desires, she feels great about herself, which helps to boost her own self-confidence. This kind of open and honest relationship increases trust and communication between the couple and brings them closer together.

It is well known that Female Led Relationships increase intimacy. Cuckolding and hotwifing give a couple the perfect chance to gain important knowledge about themselves and each other that can help heighten their level of closeness and connection. The new sexual adventures and the wide variety of options dramatically deepens a couple's bond. It provides a greater sense of sexual satisfaction for both husband and wife. Hotwifing creates a lifestyle for attaining physical satisfaction. The woman can spend quality time with men who interest her, which quenches her thirst that in more traditional marriages would typically lead to affairs and betrayals that destroy trust and relationships. One of the main benefits of Female Led Relationships is that the couple stays together because they are far more open, honest, intimate, loving, and fulfilling than many people think.

CHAPTER 25

Polyamory

People often confuse cuckolding with polyamory, but they are different. A polyamorous relationship from the Greek word *poly*, meaning "many," and Latin *amor*, meaning "love," is a non-monogamous relationship. The couple can have intimacy with multiple partners all the time, and it is an actual lifestyle. Miley Cyrus most recently made polyamory famous when she revealed that even though she was married, she is openly polyamorous. What was even more shocking was that Miley indicated her partners can be men women, gay, straight, or transgender.

Although polyamorous couples have the freedom to be non-monogamous, there are still rules laid out that are followed. A great example of this was in the movie *Savages*. All three characters lived together, and each man had sex with the main female character Ophelia, played by Blake Lively. Even the Mexican cartel characters criticized this type of living as "savage" compared to their way of killing and murdering associates in the cartel. The irony is pervasive in this movie, but it was a good portrayal of modern polyamory. The three were considered the family unit.

Cuckolding is not the same. While the woman has sex with a Bull, he is not part of the main family unit, and in general, cuckolding is not happening with a gay man or a transgender. Cuckolding is mainly about sex or humiliation, but it does not involve living and inviting others into the family unit. Polyamory may be the choice of some couples, but as Miley discovered, it's not simple. Her polyamorous ways were not shared by her husband Liam Hemsworth, and it led to their separation and divorce earlier in 2020. Their split also highlighted an extremely important point in that both the man and woman in the relationship must be on board with the lifestyle, otherwise, there will be a great deal of conflict.

I also personally feel that while cuckolding appears to be much more restrained and selective while retaining a strong bond in the main relationship, inviting and living with several people as part of the family unit represents a much more complicated situation to manage. Cuckolding can be one or two nights of fun, whereas polyamory often involves living with multiple people on a day-to-day basis. Two completely different scenarios not to be confused.

Polyamory is also growing out of economics and a shortage of straight men. Since it can be extremely expensive to live in a city, now a couple can invite a third or multiple people to live in their home, and this can lead to polyamory where they are also engaging in sex. There are numerous examples of polyamorous couples having children and living as a happy family unity. The important part is to manage the relationship among all who participate and lots of communication and consent. In the Netflix series *Narcos*, the boss of the Cali Cartel had three women he engaged with, and they all lived together happily, but his schedule with each had to be managed.

CHAPTER 26

What Is Female Led Swinging?

What's the most exciting time in life? Is it the first kiss? Dating and searching for a partner? Why is it so exciting? Is it the flirtation, suspense, and excitement of the unknown? What's going to happen during or after the date? These are the aspects missing from a long-term relationship, and if we are being honest with ourselves, we miss these moments.

So, how do you rekindle some excitement and adventure in a long-term relationship or marriage? Start dating again and meeting new people. Enter swinging and the friends with benefits lifestyle. There are more media coverage, movies, and Netflix shows coming out today on the subject than ever before. Google logs 600,000 searches a month for the term "swinging" and "friends with benefits," and there are lots of clubs, social events, and vacations available for those interested in swinging.

Katy Perry's song "I Kissed a Girl" propelled girl-on-girl experimentation into the mainstream. All of a sudden, trying it out was suddenly popular, and this is the sentiment of many couples who remain together but decide to add the experimentation and exploration of swinging into their marriages and long-term relationships. Today, women have been found to initiate swinging more often, and they are using it as an opportunity to explore their own desires. Men are loving this as they fulfill their ultimate fantasies of threesomes and multiple partners.

Swinging is becoming female led and dramatically changing things. Swinging typically refers to couples switching sexual partners with other couples, but "the lifestyle" encompasses people looking to have recreational sex or sexual experiences with anyone outside of the relationship. This might include inviting a third party for a threesome or attending sex-positive clubs or parties.

The urban dictionary describes swinging as a lifestyle of non-monogamy where sexual relations occur outside the established couple. Swingers are people who feel the need to explore and get satisfaction from others outside the primary partner. It is generally only successful when both partners engage in it with other couples, and there is complete trust and security in the relationship.

Considered part of the alternative lifestyle, swinging was often frowned upon and shunned by normal society. It was believed to be in the same realm as cheating and infidelity, but swinging couples report more happiness by following this lifestyle and generally do not get divorced. With swinging, there is no cheating, lying, and sneaking around, which often leads to trust issues. Instead, couples enjoy the night or weekend that they devote to meeting other couples, and any exploration is done with complete consent from all those involved.

Swinging is often considered safer than dating because you are not meeting strangers alone, and though there is sexual fun, swinging often leads to long-term friendships. For many, an advantage is the increased quality, quantity, and frequency of sex. Some people engage in swinging to add variety into their otherwise conventional sex lives or for curiosity. Some couples perceive swinging as a healthy outlet and means to strengthen their relationship.

Others regard such activities as merely social and recreational interaction with others. Researchers estimate that 40-50 percent of all first marriages will end in divorce or permanent separation, and about 60-65 percent of second marriages will end in divorce. Although divorce has always been a part of American society, divorce has become more common in the last 50 years. Yet swingers rarely get divorced.

Swinging involves both partners in a committed relationship sexually engaging with others for entertainment purposes and building new friendships "with benefits." Most couples in traditional conservative "patriarchal" relationships get into a "sexual rut," and where's the fun in that? A "sexual rut" is the worst rut of all because it robs you of intimacy. Swinging allows for a whole different life experience and a whole new wild world where your sexual fantasies can come true. You can escape the monotony and boredom and learn from others, hang around with fun-loving people, and of course, expand the sexual scenarios you're willing to experience with your partner.

What you must understand is that an open relationship cannot exist without openly communicating with each other. Keeping secrets and deceiving your partner about your sexual desires, needs, and activities will eventually become toxic and create feelings of neglect, insecurity, rejection, jealousy, and betrayal—all of which are sure to destroy your marriage or relationship. But this does not have to be the case. Many couples have reported the opposite. They spend more time together; they are more relaxed, happier, and sexually fulfilled.

In the swinging world, couples make their own rules around what they need within relationships and marriages and agree to abide by the boundaries they set. Couples who select this type of lifestyle seek one or many partners for the pure excitement of getting what they don't receive sexually from their primary relationship. But the primary relationship is maintained as most important, and each couple decides what is allowed and not allowed.

Swingers will often have lasting friendships with others of the opposite sex while enjoying sexual pleasures from them as well. Things never get stale, and it usually spices up the bedroom. Some couples enjoy watching other couples. They learn new tricks and techniques, and they are free to explore. After years of being together, without a lot of effort, it is almost impossible to experience the excitement and jitters you felt when you were first dating. Many dead marriages come alive when both people are free to explore their ultimate fantasies without lying, sneaking around, or cheating. And you are doing it together, which only serves to strengthen your relationship.

Women can approach swinging differently from men. Some want to experiment with women, while others need more arousal than they feel is possible with their men. Many are bi-curious, and rather than keeping these feelings bottled up inside, getting depressed, and numbing their feelings with wine every night, they are free to explore their sexuality and fantasies. Men also get the excitement and adventure they crave.

Swinging also happens with same-sex couples and is very popular with gay men. Most swingers feel that it brings more joy and fulfillment into their lives and enriches their marriages. However, they admit that swinging will not fill a void in their marriage, and this is where negative experiences can occur. Swinging will not fix a broken relationship, and if this is where you and your partner are at, you must seek the advice of a therapist.

CHAPTER 27

What Is Consensual Non-Monogamy?

S winging is part of the broader consensual non-monogamy (CNM). What is CNM exactly? Consensual non-monogamy involves couples who are married or in long-term relationships but seek to have external sexual encounters with the permission and agreement of their primary partner. So, you and your Queen are married, but you decide to explore mostly casual encounters with others. Consensual non-monogamy encompasses swinging, polyamory, or other types of open relationships.

And while consensual non-monogamy has become a hot topic, with examples cropping up everywhere in media, politics, and celebrities, the practice of a couple staying together but seeking outside physical, romantic, or emotional coupling is nothing new.

Jessica Fern, a psychologist, found that as of September 2020, about 4 percent of Americans, which is nearly 16 million people, are "practicing a non-monogamous style of relationship," and other studies show that over 21 percent of Americans engaged in consensual non-monogamy at "some point in their lifetime." In January 2020, a poll found that about one-third of US adults believe that their ideal relationship is non-monogamous to some degree.

Let's face it, we all have sexual fantasies, and sometimes we want to act on them, even when those crushes and fantasies aren't about our partner or spouse. Most of the time, we ignore our fantasies, which can go unfulfilled. For many, cheating is the only option. However, now consensual non-monogamy seems like a better option because there is more honesty and openness, and in many cases, long-term relationships and marriages remain intact. Those who engage in CNM agree on their relationship rules ahead of time, and they allow each other to have romantic and sexual relationships with others. Thus, CNM differs from monogamy in that there is a firm agreement and open acceptance to have some form of extra outside romantic or sexual relationships. The hit Netflix show *House of Cards* depicted a very solid example of CNM. The character of the First Lady, Claire, was allowed to engage in sex with a younger man, with the firm agreement of her husband, Frank, who was the President. Both people agreed to the sexual encounters.

As for personality, people who seem to engage in CNM tend to have active imaginations, a preference for variety, and a proclivity to engage in new experiences. They held more positive attitudes toward non-monogamy and greater willingness to engage in these types of open relationships. Does CNM attract people who try to avoid commitment? Studies found that highly avoidant individuals endorsed more positive attitudes toward CNM and were more willing to engage in these types of relationships.

Although avoidant people feel positive about CNM relationships, are they more likely to be in CNM relationships than monogamous relationships? In another study, people in CNM relationships reported lower levels of avoidance compared to people in monogamous relationships. Interestingly, anxiety did not differ between people in CNM and monogamous relationships, and highly anxious people had more negative attitudes toward CNM; however, anxiety was not related to the desire to engage in these types of relationships.

Non-monogamy is growing. People in consensual non-monogamous relationships report relatively high levels of trust, honesty, intimacy, and satisfaction, as well as relatively low levels of jealousy in their relationships. Ethical monogamy was derived out of the desire to change non-monogamy from being associated with the negative connotations associated with infidelity and cheating. Will Smith and Jada Pinkett are one celebrity couple of hundreds who publicly spoke about their consensual non-monogamous marriage, and today, they are still happily married. Other celebrities who admitted to enjoying the lifestyle are Gweneth Paltrow, Jessica Biel, and Thomas Middleditch.

CHAPTER 28

Open Relationships

An open relationship, also known as a non-exclusive relationship, is an intimate relationship that is sexually non-monogamous. It's a relationship involving a primary emotional and intimate relationship between two partners, who agree to at least the possibility of intimacy with other people. Open relationships include any type of romantic relationship where partners openly have sex with others outside of the primary relationship or marriage. An open relationship is where one or more parties have permission from their spouse to be romantically or sexually involved with people outside of the relationship. This is opposed to the traditional monogamous relationships where partners are exclusive.

The concept of an open relationship has been recognized since the 1970s. An open marriage is where a couple is formally married but have agreed to see other partners. In the HBO series *Succession*, the character Shiv Roy, a millionaire's daughter, writes into her marriage vows that she will have outside sexual partners while remaining married to her spouse, and he is in agreement. The fact that this topic is addressed in mainstream media, TV shows, and movies shows that open relationships are becoming more accepted. There are several different styles of open relationships. Some examples include:

- Multi-partner relationships: between three or more partners where a sexual relationship does not occur between all of the parties involved.

- Hybrid relationships: one partner is non-monogamous, and the other is monogamous.

- Swinging: falls under the category of open relationships as it involves couples engaging with other couples together.

Open relationships are synonymous with consensually non-monogamous relationships as the primary couple who are open to sexual contact with others. The most common form of open relationship is that of a married or long-term committed couple who takes on a third or sometimes fourth or fifth partner whose involvement and role in the relationship is always secondary, but there is agreement and open discussion about it. A couple practicing this relationship type might engage in sexual activity with the secondary partner together or separately, or they may each have independent outside relationships with different secondary partners—regardless of the specific parameters, the primary couple always remains a priority.

CHAPTER 29

Importance of Obedience

The role of obedience in relationships is key to creating a hierarchy of power. Obedience is a form of social influence where an individual acts in response to a direct order from another individual, who is usually an authority figure. It is assumed that without such an order, the person would not have acted in any particular way. Following commands is an essential requirement in a Female Led Relationship. A command given by the Queen to the gentleman is a demand for them to follow it without thinking or disobeying.

Why is this important? Because orders instill discipline. Orders are passed from the *Love & Obey* Mistress to the submissive man as a way of ensuring they are both on the same page. Obedience is the following of orders and plays the role of maintaining structure in the Female Led Relationship. Leadership entails commanding respect and predictable response from the obedient man. Queens have to demonstrate that they have the capacity to lead others, and they show this by their ability to successfully complete tasks.

For example, graduating from high school, college, graduate school, or working successfully in a career or as a professional. To be a *Love & Obey* Queen, a woman should demonstrate that she can run, manage, and maintain order in her relationship. As I mentioned earlier, most women who desire FLR are well-educated and smart. Often, they are better educated and smarter than their man, so this is not usually an issue.

Obedience is nothing new in society and in our interpersonal relationships. So, it's not surprising that it plays a key role in a Female Led Relationship. Many traditional cultures regard obedience as a virtue; historically, societies have expected children to obey their elders. Think about it, throughout time: in colonial America, slaves to their owners, in feudal society, serfs to their lords and lords to their king, and everyone to God. Compare the religious ideal of surrender and its importance in Islam. The word Islam literally means "surrender."

In some Christian weddings, obedience is formally included along with honor and love as part of a conventional bride's but not the bridegroom's wedding vow. In a Female Led Relationship, it is the opposite, the man vows obedience but the *Love & Obey* Mistress only promises to lead and command. As a man, you must obey your superior woman, calling her Goddess, Queen or Mistress. You should behave obediently as a child does with his mother, and if you do good, you will not have to fear any frightening punishment. Whatever your woman says to you, do as she tells you, because, through her, you will win her love and achieve happiness.

Obedience is required when your female authority figure instructs you to do something. Whereas traditional man-female roles are determined by conformity to social pressures and adhering to the norms of the majority. Obedience involves a hierarchy of power and status. The person giving the order, the *Love & Obey* Mistress, has a higher status in the relationship than the person receiving the order, the obedient gentleman. This higher status creates order, calm and creates a nurturing loving environment.

Obedience is the act of following orders without question because they come from an authority you have accepted. There are many legitimate authorities in a person's life, from parents to teachers to law enforcement and even spiritual and government leaders. Most of these authority figures mentioned above are given their authority by society. We are just told to follow what they tell us to do. In other words, we are trained to be obedient to these people. Every person at some time in their life has followed a superior without questioning why they are doing what they are doing.

For example, we never question why we take tests in school. We just take them because we are told to do so. We never question a lot of the rules that people say "are in our best interest" because they are usually told to us by someone that is in a position higher than us. In the Female Led Relationship, the woman is granted the highest position of authority and the man agrees to obey her. In exchange, he earns the right to live in a safe, loving and compassionate female led lifestyle.

Chaos is a situation of confusion and a disorderly state, lacking leadership. With an accepted authority figure and strict obedience, any guesswork on what to do goes away and reduces anxiety on how to respond in various situations. Loving female authority gives your woman control over you and she expects your obedience. Her orders and your obedience determine the positions of power that define the role of you and your woman. Once you accept your woman as your Mistress, and she accepts you as her obedient gentleman, you will see that you have eliminated elements of presumption, confusion, and incidents of confusion.

Additionally, orders establish control of various situations. Hearing your Mistress commands, you take action immediately and you follow her orders. This behavior pattern eliminates instances of second-guessing, wrong decisions, fear, and failure to follow her preferred course of action. This predictable behavior pattern also helps prevent any breakdown in communication and the relationship. Following your female's commands upholds the chain of authority. In every human institution, individuals follow a particular existing hierarchy, from the superiors to the junior staff.

In the military, for instance, the chain of command defines its leadership system. In the military, everyone has a rank and there is a chain of command. Within corporations, people have positions and jobs, from the lowest with no authority to the highest person in charge of the corporations' plan of action. It is the same in a Female Led Relationship. The failure to follow orders appears as disrespect to the Queen, which is an offense that requires punishment. She may not necessarily ask or give a clear order, but the submissive man is obliged nevertheless to obey.

Moreover, since the obedient man takes command before beginning any task, he promises to uphold the desires of the female through showing allegiance to her as his rightful leader and following her orders. The Female Led Relationship structure emphasizes the values and principles of discipline and respect for the Queen who has absolute authority. To portray these values, gentlemen have to obey and follow orders given, as they work toward achieving the female's life goals. Only with your obedience can you maintain a loving Female Led Relationship.

CHAPTER 30

Spanking and Female Led Relationships

Why is the fantasy of spanking so exciting? Men and women have both admitted to having fantasies of being tied up and whipped. More couples have admitted to engaging in spanking and adding it to their sex lives. I can recall the number of times men begged me to spank them in bed. Being a strong, fully capable woman, they were excited at the thought of being under my control, and I was fully physically capable of administering a very heavy-handed spanking that could bring even the biggest, aggressive man to tears. I could see how spanking could spice up any sex life and how it led to some very interesting and adventurous lovemaking. Men became obsessed and many of them began to almost need it to feel fully under their woman's control.

In a Female Led Relationship, the desire to be controlled by a strong female becomes even more important. More women are taking control in many aspects of their lives, and many are leading countries, governments, corporations, cities, households, and now the bedroom. My previous books *Love & Obey* and *Real Men Worship Women* are blockbuster hits and provide the essential guidance that a couple needs to

153

build a lasting, successful relationship. Part of keeping the spark alive in all relationships is to add discipline. Relationship discipline takes spanking to a whole new level in the sex life, and a better sex life naturally means a better relationship in many cases.

Why has spanking become so popular? Our desire to engage in spanking comes out of our need for attention. The only time most children get attention is when their parents are disciplining them, and maybe as adults we crave this undivided attention. Though spanking children is not advisable and outlawed, spanking in the bedroom has skyrocketed. As the leader of the *Love & Obey* and Female Led Relationship movement, I have seen how spanking has particularly become popular with women spanking men. So, I will be exploring spanking as it pertains to fun displays of discipline and dominance in the relationship.

Though spanking comes out of BDSM, this book is in no way intended to instruct on the particular practices or customs of BDSM. Here we focus on fun things the Queen can do to discipline her man in a playful respectful way if the man desires it and there is full consent. I will also touch lightly on spanking as a means of serious discipline for those couples who wish to learn more about this and, of course, how spanking can be added to as part of relationship discipline. Overall, spanking during sex is meant to add some variety and that element of fun and adventure to any relationship.

During one of the first parties I've ever attended for fetish, a massive gathering with thousands of people were moving through a maze of different rooms set up with everything to do with BDSM, bondage and torture. It was straight out of the movie Eyes Wide Shut. In one room, I observed an old man getting saran wrapped and strung up, hanging from the rafters. Three dominatrixes prepared themselves like a scene out of the movie Wonder Woman on the island of Themyscira when the female warriors were preparing for battle. Then once they were armed with their floggers, they began to flog the man while we all watched. But what I cannot stop thinking about was the smile on his face. He urged them to beat him harder and more.

They would replace their floggers for riding crops, and no matter how hard they whipped the man, he just got happier and seemed to be in a state of ecstasy. This got me thinking about the idea of spanking in the bedroom and how both the fear of what it could be, and the painful sensations wake up something primal in both men and women. Something which cannot be achieved with any other sexual act. Men who want to be dominated are intensely turned on and the women derive a great deal of satisfaction from completely controlling her man.

Think of the intense excitement you will feel when your Queen ties you up, teases you to death with role-playing, ticklers and light strokes of a whip. For some, this is a way of life. I know many couples who cannot wait to engage in some kind of dominance play and relationship discipline. Women have admitted to me the satisfaction they get when they can control their men, spank them whenever they want, and they have their men begging for more and treating them infinitely better than before.

Spanking can cause many of our deep desires for complete attention from our partners because let's face it, you need complete, undivided attention when administering and receiving a spanking. It resolves many of the disrespectful behaviors that have arisen and are accepted by society as normal, but which can lead to the unraveling and the eventual destruction of the relationship. How many times have I seen couples spending quality time together and they are on their phones or social media? Spanking in the bedroom is the one time a couple's minds do not wander, and you can't be on the phone. To partake in spanking and relationship discipline, there cannot be distractions, and this is one of the advantages to the relationship.

Within the world of dominance and submission, discipline is often eroticized and executed in a way society wouldn't otherwise condone. But many couples are waking up a dead sex life with the addition of spanking and light BDSM.

In the Female Led Relationships, more men have admitted that they enjoy and have a strong desire for their women to whip them and be aggressive. Hence, this book will deal with erotic spanking and how the Queen can administer this discipline to her man during sex. Today, more relationships are being led by women. Women are taking charge in the household and in the bedroom. Men are loving the experience of being under the spell, and the dominance of women and spanking just adds to the feeling of control for the Queen. When women feel empowered, they are at their best and men get excited when they take charge and show their power. So, it's a win-win for most.

The popularity of spanking shows no signs of slowing down. Spanking is fast becoming the favorite bedroom pastime and at 670,000 searches a month, it shows that its popularity worldwide is only growing. A recent survey showed that 75 percent of women and 66 percent of men enjoyed erotic spanking. This book will serve as an introduction to erotic spanking, and it will provide some fun ideas on how to add spanking to your sexual routine in a safe way. It cannot be understated that safety is the key as well as consent. This must always be a pastime between consenting adults who are in a committed relationship. Added to an already healthy sex life, spanking can be a fun way to spice up the bedroom while fulfilling your fantasies.

When a couple begins a female led lifestyle, they need to discuss how they want to go about it. Are they going to agree on a list of rules first, or will they agree that the female leader will train the man as she sees fit? Some couples prefer the former while others prefer the latter. Each individual couple must figure out what works for them. In my first book, *Love & Obey*, I used positive reinforcement behavioral training to encourage good behavior, and I do not endorse the use of non-consensual, physical punishment. Today, I still only endorse safe physical punishment, which is consensual and not harmful in any lasting or serious way. A couple must always fully agree before engaging in this practice and both should be adults.

I have come to see why spanking, paddling, whipping and caning is important and is such a popular and erotic form of training men, especially in a Female Led Relationship. Obedience must be demanded by the Queen, if she wishes to rule over each man. A Female Led Relationship may start out as a male sexual fantasy, but it must evolve into a real lifestyle in which the woman really leads, and the man really obeys, or it simply will not work. Spanking and relationship discipline has the ability to be a fun pastime to your sexual routine, or it has the power to transform the relationship and increase intimacy and respect.

Today, particularly in the bedroom, the tides are turning, and women (as Queens) are spanking the men. There is growing interest in spanking as more and more couples are engaging in it. Sex expert Sienna Sinclaire says, "Erotic spanking is all about spanking someone for sexual pleasure for both parties." The person being spanked enjoys it, and the person doing the spanking is also getting enjoyment.

Spanking has become so popular that now there are thousands of products available on Amazon to ensure you can create the perfect spanking experience. But is spanking during sex a new concept? Apparently not.

Today, in Female Led Relationships, many men enjoy being spanked by their Queen, and many have introduced it as an acceptable weekly—even daily—occurrence. Learning proper techniques and ways to introduce it into the sex life is key. I will be discussing all aspects of erotic spanking, including the history, proper techniques, tools, and much more. The goal of this book is to help men and women engage in fun, healthy, safe, and consensual spanking as part of their sex routine. I will also add some information on the serious practice of relationship discipline, and I will touch lightly on BDSM.

It is my wish that all couples use this as a way to build more intimacy and spice up your sex life. A healthy, fun sex life can dramatically change your relationship for the better. Spanking is a pivotal part of the Female Led Relationship where the woman administers the spanking both for fun times as well as discipline. Being the leader of the *Love & Obey* movement, which promotes a healthy and safe female led lifestyle, spanking with consent from both the Queen and her man fits perfectly into the female led world. Women are already in charge and more than capable of giving a great spanking session. Spanking has the power to transform a relationship from dull, boring, monotonous, and failing to exciting, intimate, and rewarding. Happy safe spanking. So why is spanking growing, and why is it such a turn on?

Men have been known to crave fantasies of being dominated and women love powerful men. According to a study by a new paper published in the journal *Social Psychological and Personality Science* by Joris Lammers and

Roland Imhoff, social power reduces inhibition. In other words, powerful, wealthy men are aroused by being dominated by women in bed. In one of the earliest episodes of the show Game of Thrones, Khaleesi—after taking it from her husband played by Jason Momoa—is instructed to dominate him. Once she does this, she is treated like a Queen and a Goddess.

But another study claims that power frees people from their inhibitions, and thereby increases sadomasochistic thoughts in everyone, masochistic tendencies in men who are being hurt or tortured, and sadistic thoughts in women. So, this is the reason why men crave torture and get turned on when aggressive women do this, particularly during sex.

The findings of the study showed that power increases the arousal to sadomasochism. Furthermore, the effect of power on arousal by sadistic thoughts is stronger among women than men, while the effect of power on arousal by masochistic thoughts is stronger among men than women. Masochism is defined as deriving sexual gratification from one's own pain or humiliation. As was uncovered, men crave physical torture from dominant women, which coincides with my findings as well. Men simply love the pain felt when a powerful woman smacks them on the behind, and the powerful woman is turned on by doing the act.

A 2013 study found that both dominant and submissive practitioners of BDSM were less neurotic, more extroverted, more open to new experiences, more conscientious, and less sensitive to rejection. They also had higher subjective well-being compared to the control group. This could mean two things: People with these traits are attracted to kinky sex, or kinky sex can help you grow and gain confidence.

I always think of the scene from *The Wolf of Wall Street* where Jordan Belfort is so taken with his dominatrix Venice that he was caught calling out her name in his sleep. In the scene, Venice's preferred punishment is to pour candle wax on his butt while whipping him, and he enjoys it so much that he is dreaming about it. But Mr. Belfort, a powerful head of an investment firm, craves this activity despite having access to thousands of women from all walks of life in various sexual escapades, and yet this is the one he dreams about.

There are many reasons why erotic spanking is exciting. First, there's the physical sensation. If done properly, spanking stimulates a person's genitals indirectly and creates a subtle sensation that is, no doubt, pleasurable. On the other hand, there's the psychological aspect of it. Erotic spanking can also have a lot to do with role-playing and pretend-punishment that flares up one's imagination and makes the sexual experience much more intense.

BDSM (which stands for bondage and discipline, dominance and submission, and sadism and masochism) and spanking can allow people to begin experiencing this practice in a fun way. Spanking comes out of BDSM. Discipline in BDSM is the practice in which the dominant sets rules that the submissive is expected to obey. When rules of expected behaviors are broken, punishment is often used as a means of disciplining. In BDSM, rules can be made so that a submissive or sub knows how they should behave so that the dominant is not displeased.

In Female Led Relationships, this translates into men behaving properly according to the rules of the Queen. Rules can also be for reminding subs of their inferior status, or for training a novice sub. In BDSM, when such rules are broken, punishment is often used as a means of discipline. Punishment itself can be physical such as caning, or psychological such as public humiliation or a combination of both- through bondage and spanking. So, spanking during sex extends from this practice of BDSM and discipline, which becomes a fun way for the Queen to exert her dominance over her man for both of their enjoyment.

What turns on one person about spanking is personal.

Shelby Devlin, a sex and intimacy coach, says that the person getting spanked may love the feeling of powerlessness, while another person might only be about the physical sensation. So, when you first decide you want to explore spanking, she may suggest taking time out for self-reflection. What is it about spanking that turns you and your partner on? Analyze it and discuss it.

Dawn Michael, a certified sexuality counselor and marriage and family therapist with a PhD. in human sexuality, says that being submissive or dominant with your partner can be a sexy role-play that spanking easily falls under. She says that "spanking can be a turn on for both a man and a woman who enjoy being submissive to their partner, working it into a role of submission to their Dom for a man or their master for a woman."

Men have always loved aggressive woman and spanking in sex offers the opportunity for women to take control and spice things up during sex. Imagine an entire foreplay session in which she ties you up, blindfolds you, and throws you down on the bed, and runs her flogger or horse whip all the way up from your toes to your head, then gives you a few slaps. Afterward, she gets on top and rides you to orgasm. Who can resist?

Almost everyone has some secret desire, fantasy, or fetish that turns them on in the bedroom or elsewhere. Some choose to keep their fantasies to themselves and think about them when they're alone. They consider this part of their sexuality not necessary to share. However, others have a strong urge to share their fantasy or fetish, desiring to act it out with partners. Feelings of guilt, shame, and confusion about our fantasies and what turns us on are common in our society. What is often difficult for people to understand is that sexual awakening happens when we are children. Although childhood sexuality is a natural part of development, it is often ignored in our culture, shunned, or brushed under the rug as wrong. The child is made to feel ashamed or guilty for having sexual thoughts and desires. No explanations are given, and nothing is talked about.

Women in Female Led Relationships love to give a good spanking to their men. Here's why: In spanking, there is a power exchange, and in a Female Led Relationship, the Queen is in charge. She has the power and the opportunity to exert her power on her man during sex with a little spanking. This can be a great turn-on for both men and women. Also, let's face it—dominance is sexy. Dominance during sex intensifies sexual drive, and powerful women drive men crazy. A woman in a position of power is the desire of every man, particularly to the man who has dedicated his life to serving.

Men are already submissive in a Female Led Relationship, so they have already agreed to their Queen having free reign over them. During sex, heightened levels of sexual pleasure begin once the woman assumes this role of dominance and even suggests spanking. Asserting your authority as a woman during sex portrays to the man that she knows what she wants and is going to have it. This makes her man eager to please and submit. It adds an element of adventure and fear, which can be extremely arousing.

It is normal for sex in long-term relationships to get monotonous and repetitive, so spanking shakes things up and allows the Queen to have the control, which is her deepest desire. I feel that spanking appeals to the deepest of desires of a female led woman, which is to have complete power over her man. Just as children get tired of their old toys, adults also get bored and tired of carrying out the same repetitive sexual routine and styles without the introduction of something new or adventurous.

Spanking adds an extra spice by bringing diversification in a regular sexual ritual. Spanking can make things very intimate as the Queen is in total control and the man is vulnerable in assuming positions for the Queen to spank him. Spanking brings about freshly ignited feelings that come with trying a different experience from the norm. This creates intimacy and transports you both to a whole new world and bonding you both in ways you never expected. Agreeing to introduce spanking to your sexual life is an intimate moment built. Carrying out the act together amplifies the bonding.

Many men have testified to feeling really good when they get a good spanking from their Queen. A certain stimulus is ignited when a man gets spanked because this triggers the dopamine receptors into action, bringing about sexual pleasure, which is an exciting time for both partners. It is important to not engage in kink shaming, which literally means the shaming of another person for their sexual fantasies, may happen occasionally.

Even the most compatible partners can have wildly different sexual preferences. In any sexual relationship, you're bound to be turned on by different things. That's why it's best to be kind about it when your partner tells you something they want to try in bed, even if it's not for you. Sexual fantasies are best shared as part of "dirty talk" during sex. Others may feel more comfortable bringing up the topic during more neutral times when sex isn't actually on the table.

A psychologist and certified sex therapist advised the following: Create a safe space in which you're not in overwhelmed work mode, face each other, and have eye contact. Let them know that this might be hard for you or you've been waiting for the right moment. It's also usually easier to share something with others once you've become okay with it yourself, so if this is a kink you carry unneeded shame over, it might be good to work through that shame with a sex therapist or in your own time before discussing with a partner. Additionally, it's important to remember that as long as your fantasy is between two consenting adults, it's likely to be completely normal.

A female led lifestyle involves setting up some rules for a man's behavior that his Queen can monitor. If he breaks a rule, then he knows that he must be disciplined for doing so. This discipline teaches men to behave in a more submissive, obedient, and loving way. Some couples set up rules together, while others rely on the Queen alone to create them. Some rules may be suggested by the man since he wants to work on some negative aspect of his own behavior or attitudes that he believes is holding him back from becoming a more submissive and loving man.

Some couples write down the rules, while others are quite happy to keep them on a purely verbal basis of agreement. Some men may have a tendency to debate the Queen's rules when they are called out for breaking them. This is not considered good behavior and can be disrespectful to the Queen. The most important point is consistency. If you both as a couple decide that light spanking be used when the man misbehaves, then the Queen must follow through with the spanking, and the man must obey.

Inconsistent rules are not normally a huge problem in female led households. The Queen cannot be unreasonable, but if it is agreed on, then both must follow through.

Many couples find it fairly simple and straightforward to agree on a consistent set of rules for his behavior. These rules may change and develop over time. They may be added or subtracted, as needed and common sense dictates. A Queen must create consistent consequences for his man's unruly behavior. This simply means that a Queen may spank a man briefly for a minor offense, but she may whip a man to tears for a more serious offense, ensuring that he is sobbing repentantly by the end of his punishment.

The amount and severity of the actual spanking may vary because the Queen may need to adjust these based on the man's attitude, but the relative outcomes must be consistent. Light spanking for a very minor offense, and heavy paddling with tears for a more serious offense. The consequence of a man's different types of bad behavior must be consistent, even if they are not identical. Delivering consistent consequences for male bad behavior is about maintaining the relative differences between offenses so that the reason for the punishment according to the seriousness of his bad behavior is always clear. He should know that if he gets a light spanking for an insignificant offense, he will get a severe whipping for a serious offense.

CHAPTER 31

Effects of Spanking

S panking is very exciting, and one of the effects on the body is a release of endorphins, which are responsible for happy feelings. The sensation of a hand hitting your skin can cause an adrenaline surge as additional blood flows to the surface of the skin, making all of the nerve receptors in the skin more sensitive, enhancing the sensation of a caress. The BDSM community refers to this as being a sensual experience, which shuts down the activity in your frontal cortex. It can be immensely helpful for overactive thinkers, which is why aggressive type A male personalities enjoy this. It almost calms them down.

On a physiological level, the fear element gets the adrenal glands going, flooding the system with epinephrine, followed by endorphins. Epinephrine, also known as adrenaline, energizes us when we are in the thick of "danger." Once we know the danger is over, the endorphins kick in. These are the body's natural painkillers, and they model opioids in how they make us feel by relaxing us and giving us a sense of calm and well-being.

A study from 2009 found that couples who engaged in positive, consensual sadomasochistic activity had lower levels of the harmful stress hormone cortisol and also reported greater feelings of relationship closeness and intimacy after their sexual play. And a preliminary study of a handful of "switches," like people who take on the opposite role they're used to, such as a Dom who becomes a sub, found that consensual BDSM can reduce anxiety by bringing the mind to an altered "flow" state of consciousness. This is similar to the feeling some get when they experience a "runner's high," engage in creating art, or practice yoga.

From attraction to action, sexual behavior takes many forms. At least for humans, this most basic of activities is anything but basic. As the pioneering sex researcher Alfred Kinsey put it, the only universal in human sexuality is variability itself. People normally engage in sexual activity for any number of reasons—to feel alive, to maintain a vital aspect of human functioning, to feel desirable and attractive, to achieve closeness, or to please a partner they love. Spanking adds an element of adventure and excitement to a routine sex life. The pleasure of sex arises from many factors including the release of neurochemicals, such as oxytocin and dopamine, which flood the system during orgasm, as well as the sense of connection communicated by touching.

According to Dr. Becky Spelman, a psychologist and clinical director of the Private Therapy Clinic, the reason for our appreciation of spanking is both physical and emotional. Classical conditioning is the automatic response to prior learning. For example, spanking can be linked to something you've experienced in the past. Dr. Spelman says, "It usually occurs around a particular traumatic episode, which is then stamped into the child's psyche." Spanking can cause a lot of shame in childhood, and rather than holding on to the shame, it's common for people to later in life turn the traumatic experience into a sexual one to help cope with what they have experienced, leading to a strong emotional connection between spanking and sex, which now manifests as a fetish.

When we're stressed or in pain, our brains release numerous chemicals: endorphin, serotonin, melatonin, epinephrine, norepinephrine, and dopamine. And not just physical pain but emotional and social discomfort as well—all for the purpose of rebalancing our bodies and trying to make us feel good again. One of the key players is dopamine, which is present in the body during pain and pleasure. Many agree this might be one of the reasons we can combine pain and pleasure in a single situation. Spanking causes all of this to go on in our bodies at the same time.

For your man, as a submissive after the initial opiate-like euphoria wears off, many subs feel what's often called a "drop" or a "sub drop." This is when the biochemicals begin to taper off, leaving a sleepy, relaxed feeling in their place. At this point, what's known as "aftercare," in which the sub's physical and emotional needs are seen to, is very important. After the exertion of play, for instance, a blanket or robe may be needed since the body temperature often drops from the sudden stoppage of energy.

The reason for the spanking is because when it is done on the butt, its proximity to the sex organs makes it part of the overall sexual feeling. During the spanking, the gluteal muscles are often squeezed together, which researchers have found is similar to what happens during orgasm. Sexual peaks are achieved when blood flow increases and collects in key hot spots or erogenous zones.

In the case of the male, the proximity of the buttocks to the scrotum and the penis is an important factor and seems to contribute to the erection. Blood rushing to the spanked bottom causes the male sexual organs to swell, much as they do in preparation for the orgasm. An additional anatomical element in sexual response to spanking is the fact that the anal opening shares some muscles with the perineum—a very erogenous area between the anus and the genitalia. During the course of most spankings, this area comes into contact with either the hand or the tool used to strike the buttocks.

Occasionally, depending on the size of the paddle or spanking implement, the sexual organs will be accidentally struck—this can happen with either gender as the recipient. While no damage is sustained, an immediate sexual response is often the result. One phenomenon is the apparent fact that the sexual feelings induced by a spanking are either stronger than or blot out the presence of pain. While there may be some physical discomfort, it adds to the eroticism of this activity rather than detracting.

The Thrill of the Spank

The emotional and psychological aspects of pain and pleasure involve submission (giving up control to another person), humiliation (a form of psychological pain), sexual objectification (the sexual value of the body as an object), and role-playing (participating in sexual fantasies).

Whether it's good for the man or not, psychologically speaking, some people like to give a good spanking. Power is a rush, in fantasy and reality, and spanking, even at a birthday party, gives you a certain power—the power to hurt, humiliate, heal, or stimulate. Of course, power corrupts, especially in real life. For example, many people pursue physical power over others, often entering politics, police, or military careers, and "spanking" the populace with punitive laws and sadistic punishments—not to mention "spanking" smaller, relatively defenseless countries with bombs.

Others prefer to keep their power trips in their erotic imaginations or perhaps act them out through real-life role-play. Some cultivate spanking as an art, deriving as much creative pleasure from giving a good spanking as a musician might from playing an instrument. And yes, there's a fine line between making music and making love—and no, it's not just because one of my favorite forms of spanking is Butt Bongo.

Dominance is traditionally considered a male prerogative, so it is most popular among young men who are relatively powerless in real-life society—perhaps by choice, though usually they may not even have any testosterone-pumping energy to spare. But more and more women are saying that they enjoy being dominant, "on top," and wielding a whip or even sprouting a penis (okay, Freud was right about some women having "penis envy"). This "penis" could be the obvious strap-on dildo, which many dominant women enjoy sporting, but the penis substitute could also be a phallic foot (as in the Bible, where the foot, leg, or thigh is often used as a euphemism for the forbidden-to-pronounce male sex organ), or a hand, paddle, whip or flogger.

Often as subtle as it is predictable, desire is part biology, part psychology, and takes shape differently in men and women. For men, arousal typically precedes desire. But for women, desire precedes arousal, in response to physical intimacy, emotional connection, and an atmosphere free of distractions and everyday concerns. Scientists are continuously exploring the interplay of biological influences, such as neurohormones that suppress or enhance desire, and psychological influences, such as emotions and relationships. Spanking affects a man's arousal, leading to more desire of his Queen to control him, which eventually leads to both being more turned on.

Indeed, besides so-called disciplinary, erotic, and sensual spanking, there is also therapeutic spanking, or "spanking therapy," which is employed for its curative effects. The therapeutic power of a spanking or flogging may be primarily physical, like a good massage or brisk rubdown, but spanking therapy can also be deeply psychological, releasing the man being spanked from all kinds of stress, guilt, shame, and tension, with much of it stemming from childhood. The best spanking therapy breaks through destructive, debilitating mental and sexual blocks, improving the mental well-being of both the man getting spanked and his Queen.

In 2005, a team of Russian scientists led by Sergei Speransky found "whipping therapy" to be an effective prophylaxis against alcohol and drug abuse, depression, suicidal thoughts, and psychosomatic diseases due to the release of endorphins during and after spanking. Dr. Speransky recommends 30 sessions of 60 whip lashes on the buttocks in every session for maximum therapeutic effect. Today, the Queen spanking her man even during sex can serve as therapy.

CHAPTER 32

BDSM

B DSM is the acronym for bondage, discipline, submission, masochism, and it's an ancient practice. According to research, there's evidence of BDSM sex practices in ancient Greek art, and the Kama Sutra, which was written in 300 AD, publicized erotic spanking as a way to add a little something extra to people's sex lives. Although, the number of participants will remain a mystery.

Unfortunately, BDSM has been misunderstood. Italian researchers recently surveyed the sexuality of 266 Italian men and women who enjoy bondage, discipline, and sadomasochism (BDSM). The study population ranged in age from 18 to 74, with an average of 41. The researchers also surveyed 200 demographically similar men and women not involved in BDSM. The two groups reported similar feelings about their sexuality, but the BDSM individual reported less sexual distress and greater erotic satisfaction. The researchers said they hoped their study would reduce the stigma associated with it.

BDSM has emerged from the underground and is now out in the open. It involves a power exchange and has the potential to make relationships more sexually fulfilling, but like all relationships, it's a matter of communicating wants and desires. And like in other bad relationships, abuse and manipulation can happen, but that is a matter of individual personalities and relationships, not a characteristic of BDSM as a whole.

Psychologist Kasi Alexander says, "It's important to make a distinction between mental conditions and different sexual preferences and alternative lifestyles. The most important aspect of the mental disorder consideration is the difference between true sadism and kinky sadism." A vast majority of "sadists" in the BDSM community derive no pleasure from inflicting pain unless the recipient is enjoying the experience, whereas a true sadist is not concerned with the other person's benefit.

People are not talking about it more openly than they did in the past, but they're also practicing BDSM in their sex lives. According to OkCupid's 2015 Hangover report, 58 percent of users have a desire to participate in bondage. But how many actually do? *Psychology Today* explores a variety of questions such as: What kinds of personality types engage in BDSM? Do people who engage in BDSM come from abusive families? Why would someone want to engage in BDSM play? Is BDSM abuse? Are BDSM relationships cold, distant, controlling, or abusive? What kind of feelings do people who engage in BDSM experience before, during, and after intense sensation play?

The magazine also conducted a study involving more than 200 participants who engage in BDSM. Information was obtained from respondents via an online survey, consisting of roughly twelve qualitative questions about the individual's motivations and experiences engaging in BDSM, as well as three psychological instruments: the Experiences in Close Relationships Scale-Short Form (ECR-S), which measures attachment style; the Adverse Childhood Experiences Scale

(ACE), which measures the level of childhood trauma, and the Big Five Inventory (BFI), which measures personality traits.

The findings were as follows: No significant difference between people who engage in BDSM and those who don't in traumatic childhood experiences, such as feeling neglected, having divorced or separated parents, witnessing the abuse of a parent, or living with substance or alcohol abusers. People who engage in BDSM had significantly higher scores on the BFI openness to new experiences. Last, there is no significant difference between people who engage in BDSM and people who don't in Anxious or Avoidant Attachment Styles. This means that BDSM participants are not more likely than others to be uncomfortable with closeness in relationships or are more likely to be the needy stalker type.

To summarize, those who practice BDSM do not have more pathological personality traits or insecure attachment styles or substantially more adverse childhood experiences. And neither are most of them experiencing negative feelings nor being driven by harmful motivations in their engagement of intense sensation play.

While the extent people exploring the realms of BDSM will vary from couple to couple, even some of the "vanilla" sex people have probably picked up a blindfold and at least considered integrating it into their sex lives. In 2015, Indiana University researchers surveyed a representative sample of 2,021 American adults. Many said they had tried some elements of BDSM as revealed in the following statistics: 30 percent spanking, 22 percent dominant/submissive role-playing, 20 percent restraint, and 13 percent flogging.

In 2017, Belgian scientists surveyed 1,027 Belgian adults of which 47 percent admitted to experimenting with BDSM. Thirteen percent said they experimented that way regularly. Eight percent said they felt committed to BDSM sexuality.

BDSM is all about discipline in which the goal is to teach the sub that they have made a mistake for the purpose of learning self-restraint and becoming a better sub in the future. The punishment is typically related to the mistake and is proportionate to the severity and frequency of the mistake. In BDSM, two things must not be confused—the disciplining of the sub and sadomasochism (S&M), involve giving pain or torture to a "sub" for sexual enjoyment.

Contrarily, punishments for disciplining are in response to violations of predetermined rules or for otherwise displeasing the dominant. Punishment is considered necessary, because without it, a sub may repeat mistakes and thus not improve in their role. So, spanking during sex would be considered a lighter version of both branches of BDSM, but it should not be considered a pure version as there is a serious art and practice of BDSM to be followed. But since erotic spanking has emerged from BDSM, it is fun to explore. The man is the sub, and the woman is the Queen and dominant.

In spanking role-play, the Queen must administer a spanking for her man's disobedience. A fun way to do this is if you disrespect your Queen in any way, such as making fun of her, failing to listen to her or abide by her rules, then she can command you to stand up, pull down your pants, and give you a sweet spanking before leading to sex. Some couples enjoy just giving the spanking as a daily discipline, and others prefer to begin with the spanking, which can lead to being so turned on you must have hot passionate sex after this.

Some Commonly Used Terms in BDSM:

Aftercare: Aftercare is post-play etiquette in which all parties check in on one another to ensure the scene was enjoyable, tend to any bruises as well as emotional needs, and communicate how all parties feel.

BDSM: Stands for Bondage, Discipline, Sadism, and Masochism; an umbrella term for any kinky play that involves a consensual power exchange.

Bondage: Bondage is when one partner (typically the submissive) is tied up by the dominant partner. Bondage is frequently part of impact play because tying up the submissive, who then consensually can't move, adds to the thrill of the scene.

Dom Drop and Sub Drop: During a BDSM scene, endorphins and adrenaline run high for all partners. As a result, like a crash from a drug, both the submissive and dominant partner may experience a comedown immediately after or even a few days later. All parties involved have a responsibility to tend to their partner during their drop.

D/S: Refers to dominance and submission. Typically, one partner takes on the dominant or top role. In impact play, this is the person inflicting the spanks or other forms of play. The submissive is the bottom or the person receiving the impact on their body.

Edge play: Edge play refers to BDSM activities that push the limit of what is considered safe, sane, and consensual. This often refers to activities involving bodily fluids and blood. Single-tail whips are considered a form of edge play as they can draw blood and inflict harm if not used correctly.

Hard Limits: Your hard limits are activities that are absolutely off-limits and should be communicated to your partner prior to play.

Kink: A kink refers to any sexual interest that is outside the heterosexual vanilla norm.

Pain Slut: Pain sluts are people who enjoy erotic pain.

Play: Play is a word used within the kink community to refer to any erotic activity, from penetrative intercourse to impact play.

RACK: Stands for Risk-Aware Consensual Kink and is the guideline all kinky play should follow. It means all parties understand the risks they are taking and consent.

Safe word: A safe word is a word agreed upon by all parties that indicates it's time to immediately stop the play. A safe word is used instead of "stop" or "no," as some people enjoy scenes in which they consensually "fight back."

SCC: Stands for Safe, Sane, and Consensual. It is another acronym for safety guidelines, although RACK is more commonly used today because what is considered safe and sane varies from person to person.

Scene: A scene refers to the time in which the agreed upon kinky play occurs.

Soft Limits: Soft limits are things that you are curious about but hesitant to try. Perhaps in the future you'll want to try them, but as of now, it's a no. Your limits may change with time.

Corporal punishment is a form of physical punishment that involves the deliberate infliction of pain as retribution for an offense. It is used to discipline or reform a wrongdoer or to deter attitudes or unacceptable behavior. The term usually refers to methodically striking the offender with an implement, whether in judicial, domestic, or educational settings.

Different parts of the anatomy may be targeted, such as the buttocks—whether clothed or bare—have often been targeted for punishment, particularly in Europe and the English-speaking world.

The advantage is that these fleshy body parts are robust and can be chastised accurately, without endangering any bodily functions, and they also heal well relatively quickly. In some cultures, punishment applied to the buttocks entails a degree of humiliation, which may or may not be intended as part of the punishment. Hitting the back of the thighs and calves is at least as painful, if not more so, but this can cause more damage in terms of scars and bruising. The upper back and the shoulders have historically been a target for whipping (e.g., in the UK with the cat-o'-nine-tails in the Royal Navy and some pre-1948 judicial punishments), and today generally in the Middle East and the Islamic world. The soles of the feet are extremely sensitive and flogging them has sometimes been done in the Middle East.

Flagellation also falls under the umbrella of BDSM, and this is the act of spanking. It involves flogging, whipping, or lashing in which one is beating the human body with special implements such as whips, lashes, rods, switches, and the cat o' nine tails. Typically, flogging is imposed on an unwilling subject as a punishment; however, it can also be given willingly or performed on oneself in religious or sadomasochistic contexts. Usually, it is the butt or back that is struck, but for a moderated subform of flagellation, described as bastinado, the soles of a person's bare feet are used as a target for beating.

In some circumstances, the word "flogging" is used loosely to include any sort of corporal punishment, including birching and caning. Today, women are now freer to assert their dominance over men, and men cannot resist a strong woman. Furthermore, many men welcome discipline from their Queens. Strong women are perceived as exciting, and anything can happen. Bad girls are the ones who will throw a man down, tie him up, strip off his pants, and tease him until he can't stand it anymore. Who can resist giving up all of the power to a sexy, dominant woman who is fully capable of taking charge? Also, an unstable hierarchy can cause men considerable anxiety. However, an established chain of command, such as those practiced by the military and many workplaces, reduces testosterone and curbs male aggression. When a man knows his Queen is in charge and agrees, he will be calmer and easier to deal with.

In *Psychology Today*, after looking into the mating preferences of more than 5,000 men and women by way of survey, researcher and biological anthropologist Helen Fisher, Ph.D., writes that men desire smart, strong, successful women. Her article showed that 87 percent of men said they would date a woman who was more intellectual than they were, who was better educated, and who made considerably more money than they did, while 86 percent said they were in search of a woman who was confident and self-assured.

Strong women go after the things they want in life. They don't sit by and wait for love to fall into their lap. They're not afraid to flirt and show a true interest, but they also define what they want in a relationship. They let a man know right away if they're looking for a simple hookup or if they're after a real relationship, and they don't stick around if a guy wants something different. Men don't have to guess with strong women, and they can sit back and let her make the first move and take control. This is the opposite of most other areas of life in which they must compete. With a woman in charge, they are free to allow her to lead and make decisions. This also makes the woman happier, and a happier woman is a much sexier woman.

CHAPTER 33

Role-Play

R ole-play during sex involves acting out a sexual fantasy. It may be done during foreplay, or it can be the main event. According to the 2015 Sexual Exploration in America Study, more than 22 percent of sexually active adults engage in role-playing. Couples love role-play as a chance to spice up their sex life and try new things or be someone else. This tends to be sexually arousing because suddenly you and your partner can perform acts out of the norm.

Spanking presents a perfect time to use role-play because the Queen becomes a character who is spanking her man as the submissive character. Some couples become so involved in role-playing they insist on elaborate costumes and scripts. Many fetish parties will act out role-playing fantasies, but they can just as easily be done at home.

Nearly any role could become the base material for an erotic experience, and there is no limit to what objects an individual could consider sexual. It may, for example, involve wearing a costume that is regarded as erotic, such as a miniskirt and stockings, or one or both partners being nude, say for an evening. It may involve elements of dominance and submission, passivity, or obedience. It may involve sexual bondage, with either partner being restrained. Bondage plus spanking go together perfectly.

Another element that makes sexual role-play appealing is that the concept of it is not only about the physical act of getting off. It's actually just as stimulating for the mind as it is for the body.

When the Queen and her man are able to truly let go in order to fulfill their deepest fantasies in the form of role-playing, it taps right into the imagination, which, in turn, creates an even sexier physical experience.

Some of the exciting role-playing games include:

1. Doctor or nurse and patient

2. Teacher and student

3. Escort and client

4. Boss and employee

5. Housewife and handyman (plumber or carpenter)

6. Master and slave

7. Photographer and model: this allows one partner to photograph the other as a precursor to sexual interaction.

8. Female villain and James Bond

9. CIA agent and criminal

10. Strangers in a bar

Here are some tips on how to make your role-playing spectacular.

The best way to start something new is to discuss it with your partner, so you are both excited about it and can come up with fantasies that will stimulate both of you. You want to ensure you are both comfortable and willing to add it to your sex life. Not everyone likes to add new things to sex. Many people are quite happy with normal, so it is important to ensure both of you are eager.

As the Queen in a Female Led Relationship, this may be something you wish to add to your sex sessions and your man is obligated to follow your lead. But it is important to respect his ideas as well. If it is the man who must convince the Queen, be respectful and make your suggestions but allow her to make the final decision. This is why communication becomes crucial.

Role-playing doesn't need to be complicated. You can start by doing some smaller and simpler things to get each other going. This could be wearing lingerie or trying out a sex toy. Heck, the two of you could even test out by speaking in some accents or using different props. Start simple and then move to complicated. Once you have done it a few times, then you can move to create more complicated scenarios. This is the point when you can add spanking and combine the two.

Remember, role-play should be fun. It may feel awkward and intimidating at first, but it's worth it to just try it out. The best way to figure out what works for you and your man is simply to try it out.

CHAPTER 34

How to Make the Perfect Playroom

One of the greatest ways to make your spanking and sex sessions so much more exciting is to set up a playroom—*Fifty Shades of Grey* style. There is a reason we were so excited when Christian Grey led Ana into the most luxurious playroom. A sex playroom becomes a special place for better sex, more relaxation, and a greater connection with your partner. A Queen can really feel like royalty in a playroom.

A playroom can enhance the sexiness of your sex and spanking sessions. In *Fifty Shades of Grey,* Christian has Ana sign contracts before entering the playroom, which had every type of equipment for play artistically laid out, resembling a kinky hotel room in Las Vegas. A bench with restraints, the cross, even a swing contraption have been used. The whips can range from a very sturdy paddle or leather flogger and whips. Some couples get into monogrammed restraints and creative garb. One great example is the *Eyes Wide Shut* capes. The Goddess and her man wear these sumptuous capes until it's time to start spanking when then man drops his cape and bears his naked body.

Red and black are the most popular colors or something regal with rich purples, yellows, and blues. Lighting doesn't need to be dark, but it can be. Soft and romantic, harsh spotlights, or disco balls can all create a fun scene.

Here are some great sex dungeon toys, accessories, and furniture:

Sex Swing: A sex swing is such a great addition to a dungeon, and you don't have to fasten it to the ceiling with a large screw. Some are built to fit on a door jamb and are versatile enough to accommodate several different positions.

Blackout Mask: If you cannot fully black out your windows, a blackout mask is a great way to create atmosphere and suspense. It's a great feature to keep hanging on your dungeon wall.

Cuffs: A dungeon wouldn't be complete without having a set of handcuffs on hand to restrain your partner. If you have a bed, you can keep them near it. You can place your partner's wrists above their head. Better yet—if you are doing some bed play or even floor play, suction cuffs are an awesome option for restraint.

Collar and Leash: Your bottom/submissive might like to be led around by the collar in a session. In that case, you can install a hook on the wall and hang a collar and leash to use in your dungeon.

Spanking Paddle: Tools for pain play can be a big part of your dungeon play. There are so many to choose from, from whips to floggers to canes.

Storage: Choosing the right storage is important so you can have easy access to your tools and store them away carefully. One way to organize and store your tools when not using them is to install hooks on the walls of your dungeon. This not only helps keep you organized but having them out on display can set the psychological tone you may want for your submissive.

Here are some fun furniture you can add:

Spanking Bench

The spanking bench, or spanking horse, is a piece of furniture used to position your man on it, with or without restraints. Even celebrities like Cara Delevingne and Ashley Benson have reported buying and using a sex bench. Cara has previously hinted at an interest in BDSM during an interview on RuPaul's podcast *RuPaul: What's the Tee?* The spanking bench is similar to a sawhorse with a padded top and rings for restraints.

What's nice about it is that it allows the Queen to move around her subject easily, choosing to taunt and tease him from any angle. With restraints, it will ensure your man is held in place and he is comfortable. Some couples have these custom made with luxurious materials or high-quality leather. It creates the ability to explore a multitude of sexual positions, and it can also be easily folded up and stored away since it is also designed to be discreet.

Sex Couch

A sex couch is the ultimate, classic sex lounge chair. It's designed so you can sit on it in a variety of ways so you can get that perfect position. Many come with straps and extra pillows to prop yourself up further or to have bondage furniture.

BDSM Bondage Board

Bondage frame boards and tables are adjustable, so you can strap or rope a person to the board. This table has convenient holes with access points for the face, nipples, and genitals, and it is collapsible, so you can store it under the bed or in a closet. It makes for a great addition to any playroom.

Bondage Cross

A bondage cross is a standing fixture that allows you to strap someone in a vertical position. It's a stark fixture for your burgeoning sex dungeon...or an interesting, abstract sculpture in the living room that your Uncle Joe might ask about. The cross above is designed with vinyl upholstery and hand-welded aluminum, so you're getting the top-of-the-line as far as bondage furniture is concerned.

Here are some added tips:

Choose furniture that is high-quality and well made, even if it's just one or two pieces. Make sure floors, walls, furniture, and other surfaces are easily cleaned and sanitized.

If you're going to use candles for wax play or just decoration, nearby fabrics should be flame retardant. Battery candles can be convincing enough if you want mood lighting without worrying about the fire department showing up. Carpeted floors might not be the best idea, especially if you're going to be dealing with sweat, drool, and other bodily functions. Area rugs are the go-to if you want something soft under your feet. Wood items should be sanded to avoid splinters. It's important to keep your playroom safe, warm, comfortable, and clean.

CHAPTER 35

Transition from Patriarchy to Female Led

O ne of the biggest issues that can arise in relationships is the transition from going from Patriarchy to Female Led. How can men really learn to do something if they feel it may go against their nature? You've been taught to take control and "be a man," be strong and assertive all of your life, and now, with times changing and a desire to serve your Queen, you must adapt and change. I recognized a long time ago that real change in relationships can be the most difficult undertaking. Even therapy without practicing the principles learned can result in failure.

Have you ever come across a strong woman who seemed perfect relationship material but after a few dates, you could tell that you just didn't feel the same level of attraction as you felt originally for her? And you really wanted to take things to the next level, but for some reason, you can't seem to show a similar intention and you didn't know what to do about it? Or do you often struggle to keep her interest for long? Have you ever slept with a woman too soon only to realize that she has almost disappeared from your life for no apparent reason? And does it happen a lot even when you know it shouldn't be happening? Or are you in a relationship where you don't know how to commit further and take it to the next level? And you always ask yourself: Why isn't my relationship moving forward?

Every time you think about this subject, you want to avoid dealing with it because it makes you even more distant and withdrawn to the point where you fear your Queen might leave you? Are you feeling absolutely helpless and frustrated because you want to make her understand how much you want to be with her? You could be holding yourself back with past conditioning and making it impossible to relax and enjoy your new Female Led Relationship.

This is where *Love & Obey* affirmations can create a turning point and provide a real purpose. It is time to make service to your Queen a priority by changing your thinking and conditioning with these daily affirmations. I recognized a long time ago, after writing my second book *Real Men Worship Women*, that men need rules to follow in order to create the right relationship groundwork and to get through the transition.

If men understand these rules early on, then there will be less conflict, stress, and anxiety in the transition stage. This transition is the period when a man may desire change, but he must also change his way of thinking, which has been ingrained in him from youth. Properly worshipping the Queen requires reprogramming at the subconscious level, along with following all of the rules daily. When a man has achieved reprogramming, the woman is going to feel more confident and relaxed. Both you and your Queen can be relaxed. Once you have reprogrammed your patriarchal thinking, it will be easier to address the Queen as supreme.

Speech is important in Female Led Relationships. A man must obey his woman in his speech, calling her Goddess,

Queen, or Mistress. "Yes, Queen, of course, my Goddess." "As you command, my Queen." By adding speech in the form of affirmations to worship her daily, you can change past conditioning. Female led will become as normal as brushing your teeth and flossing. The more ingrained a female led life is in men, the fewer disagreements and the more opportunity to create a deeper, more intimate connection. You will repeat things like "I obey my Queen," "My life is to love, obey, and serve the Queen," and "I will honor and respect my Queen each and every day." Every great institution has an honor code—it's the extra layer of accountability. Turning point affirmations are like your honor code, when you say use them with real intention, you create changes in you and your approach to female led life and your Queen.

The breakdown in relationships occurs when women and men are unsure of their roles, and this struggle can exist when couples focus overly on "equality" in a relationship. There is no equality in governments or organizations and rarely is it achieved in relationships. How often does anything get accomplished if everyone in the firm is equal and there is no leader? Usually never. The same is true in relationships. Women have allowed themselves to believe that the best they can hope for is equality. The pursuit of equality eventually leads to disagreement and power struggles.

At some point, one person needs to step up and take the lead. For years, the man was expected to take on that role, but today, in a Female Led Relationship, the Queen needs to take leadership in making the decisions and managing the day-to-day activities. There is a reason the saying, "Happy wife, happy life," exists. When the Queen is happy, you, as the supportive gentleman, will be happy too. The challenge occurs when a man must change his thinking on a deeper level.

Perhaps you are just discovering female led life but you have been conditioned to be patriarchal. Many men are raised by women, but having divorced parents tend to affect how men will view their position in relationships. Men may have a desire to submit, but desire and doing this daily with their Queens can be problematic. This is where reprogramming comes in and affirmations can be beneficial.

Affirmations are used to reprogram the subconscious mind and encourage us to believe certain things about ourselves or about the world and our place within it. They are also used to help us create the reality we want. *Love & Obey* affirmations will help you through this transition. You will reprogram much of your old ways of thinking, and you can practice these affirmations at any time. In the morning, during sex or during a meditative break. Female led affirmations are designed to help you get rid of the chains of the old patriarchal conditioning that often prevents men from being truly present in their relationships.

CHAPTER 36

Female Led Affirmations

F emale led affirmations are specifically for the purpose of helping men accept female led life and the Queen as being in charge. Affirmations are becoming more popular, and they have seen significant use in many aspects of mental reprogramming for health, stress management, well-being, and now, relationships. Affirmations seem simple on the surface—just repeat a couple of lines, but they are, in fact, a powerful method to control specific areas of the brain that can bring about significant transformation.

Many gurus and spiritual leaders swear by affirmations, and they have become an important part of many programs. For hundreds of years, the wisdom teachings of the East have utilized methods for the study and transformation of the mind-body.

Mindfulness Training provides instruction in meditation, mind-body healing, and affirmations from both a psychological and spiritual perspective. Reprogramming is real and can be used in relationships. The Female Led Relationship is powerful, but for many couples, there are challenges when a man must transition to his new role of a supportive gentleman. Men have varying degrees of success with getting through this transition; however, many encounter difficulties when they must get to the deeper levels of serving their Queens.

I recognized many years ago that men were major supporters of female led life. More men would contact me on a daily basis requesting guidance on how to create a better Female Led Relationship. However, they were also the ones who expressed difficulty with fully committing and showing submission. I realized that one of the greatest achievements would be to help men with their transition from patriarchal thinking to female led life.

Love & Obey affirmations are yet another tool that can help men with their desire to serve. The more you can align your mental desire to serve with action, the more success you will have in your Female Led Relationship. Most women are already chomping at the bit and eager to take charge. Many couples experience some growing pains when the female is demanding proper service from her man, but he is not completely capable of submitting to her. Yes, it can take some time to adjust, or it takes fully immersing yourself in learning to love, obey, and serve her.

Neuroscience shows us that every minute of every day, our body is physically changing in response to the thoughts that run through our head. Just thinking about something causes your brain to send signals and release neurotransmitters. These chemicals control virtually all of your body's functions, including your mood and feelings. Over time and with repetition, via neuroplasticity, it's been proven that your thoughts change your brain, your cells, and even your genes. What you think, visualize, and say to yourself can change your body, brain, and life.

One way to harness this power to help you is through affirmations. Studies suggest that positive affirmations can help us respond in a less defensive and resistant way when presented with life challenges. For example, a significant challenge is experiencing changes in the relationship. When men attempt to live out their fantasy with a strong demanding woman, they need guidance and instruction on how to navigate their new purpose of submitting and serving their Queen. My books *Love & Obey* and *Real Men Worship Women* provided the rules and general instructions on how to properly worship the Queen.

Now, *Love & Obey* affirmations will help to make this instruction much more natural as it becomes a part of your normal thinking. You will no longer be drawn to patriarchal tendencies, but rather, you will begin to think like a fully supportive gentleman. The reason this is so powerful is that subconscious, ingrained conditioning can surface and affect your behavior in relationships. The more you can reprogram your mind to serve your Queen and view her as supreme, the fewer conflicts will arise and this translates into more happiness in your relationship.

Affirmations were made popular by gurus like Napoleon Hill, the author of *Think and Grow Rich*, who went on to sell millions of copies of his self-help programs. Most of his books were promoted as expounding principles to achieve "success." Another extremely successful book and program that uses affirmations is *The Secret,* which promoted "the Law of Attraction" using affirmations. It was so successful it has sold over 30 million copies worldwide and translated into 50 languages. There is no doubt that affirmations change lives, and when used correctly, they will help you and your Queen create the perfect Female Led Relationship. By directing your thoughts, these affirmations will help put into the vibration for attracting your desires.

The first step in manifesting is to be clear as to what you want. Most people are not able to form a clear concise picture of what they truly desire, and this is a necessary step in using affirmations to create the turning point and your new perfect Female Led Relationship. You must visualize what your desired life looks like. Believe it is indeed happening as you repeat the affirmations. Then you need to trust the process and show gratitude and acceptance for your Queen and your desired new relationship or marriage. Only when careful attention to this is done daily will you witness an amazing transformation.

How Affirmations Work

Self-affirmation theory suggests that people have a fundamental motivation to maintain self-integrity, perceive themselves as good, virtuous, and predict and control imperative outcomes. In virtually all cultures and historical periods, there are socially shared conceptions of what it means to be a person of self-integrity. Having self-integrity means that one perceives oneself as living up to a culturally specific conception of goodness, virtue, and agency. Self-affirmation theory examines how people maintain self-integrity when this perception of the self is threatened.

Changing patriarchal conditioning, which has been deeply ingrained for years, can affect self-integrity. Personal regard is related to self-integrity. Researchers have examined the psychology of the importance of people's sense of personal regard. Some have suggested that a sense of personal regard emerges early in an infant's life and remains relatively stable throughout the lifetime. They have also documented the various adaptations people deploy to maintain self-regard. The social psychologist Daniel Gilbert and his colleagues have suggested that people have a psychological immune system that initiates psychological adaptations to threats to self-regard.

Indeed, these protective adaptations may lead to rationalizations and even distortions of reality. When self-integrity is threatened, according to self-affirmation theory, people need not defensively rationalize or distort reality. Instead, they can reestablish self-integrity through affirmations. Affirmations are positive statements used to challenge negative, depressing, or anxiety-producing thoughts and beliefs. They can also just be general supportive thoughts providing encouragement. Think of daily affirmations as exercising the mind. Affirmations reinforce an intention so deeply that it bypasses one's conscious mind and goes straight into the subconscious. This is powerful because the subconscious mind believes what it is told, much like a blank screen that displays whatever is projected onto it.

Repeating affirmations helps to reprogram the unconscious mind for success. It helps eliminate negative and limiting beliefs and transforms your comfort zone from a limited one, keeping you trapped in mediocrity to a more expanded one where anything is possible. Affirmations are used to influence your thinking patterns, behavioral habits, health, and moods. Affirmations come out of self-affirmation theory contending that if individuals reflect on values that are personally relevant, they are less likely to experience distress and react defensively when confronted with information that contradicts or threatens their sense of self.

People's attempt to protect self-integrity may threaten the integrity of their relationships with others. Yet, these normal adaptations can be turned off through a psychological adaptation to threat, an alternative adaptation that does not hinge on distorting the threatening event to render it less significant. One way that these defensive adaptations can be reduced, or even eliminated, is through the process of self-affirmation. This makes them perfect for reprogramming for something as serious as a relationship, which affects so much of our lives.

Affirmations are aligned with Freud's explanation of the conscious mind as the tip of the iceberg with the subconscious and unconscious beneath that allows us to discuss affirmations and their impact on behavioral changes by accessing the subconscious to drive the conscious behavior. Imagine that the subconscious mind is like a computer drive. It sorts every thought, action, and memory, and over time, the drive gets cluttered and the "files" become corrupted, with some files appearing more dominant than others.

In our subconscious mind, these files can relate to negative influences in our environment, messages from powerful authoritarian figures, bad habits we pick up over time, chronic stress, and ingrained habits related to food choices. Positive thinking and our subconscious mind work with health issues. For one study, cancer survivors reported that participants with higher optimism reported better health, greater happiness, and hopefulness. Affirmations were also found to affect cardiovascular functioning.

At the behavioral level, self-affirmation improves problem-solving performance on tasks related to executive functioning. Numerous studies highlight that thinking about self-preferences activate neural reward pathways. A group of researchers found that self-affirmation would activate brain reward circuitry during functional MRI studies. Their findings suggest that self-affirmation may be rewarding and may provide a first step toward identifying a neural mechanism that may produce beneficial effects. By enhancing the psychological resources of self-integrity, the act of self-affirmation reduces defensive responses to threatening information and events, leading to positive outcomes.

CHAPTER 37

Change Patriarchal Conditioning

Many relationships begin to unravel when there is too much unhealthy conditioning happening which is why it is necessary for you to change patriarchal conditioning in order for your Female Led Relationship to thrive. For example, you have been together with your partner for a while and have developed poor communication habits. With increasing arguments and disagreements, you both just ignore it.

Psychologist Patricia Evans discusses negative conditioning that occurs in relationships. She tells the story of a scientist who uses two frogs to study the effects of conditioning. The scientist places the first frog in a pan of hot water. The frog immediately jumps out. She places the second frog in a pan of cold water while the scientist gradually turns up the heat. The frog doesn't move. The scientist gradually turns up the heat again. The frog continues to stay. The scientist continues to turn up the heat, and yet again, the frog stays. Finally, the scientist turns up the heat to a boiling point. The frog continues to stay until it's boiled to death. This is similar to abuse, which often starts out slowly, and gradually picks up speed and intensity.

Unfortunately, this pattern can continue unending for years and years. Slowly, day by day, a person's soul gets chipped away. One day the person wakes up and realizes he/she has been sitting in a pan of boiling water. The reason conditioning is a powerful part of all relationships is that it can hinder progress, particularly when it is necessary to make major changes in having to create a Female Led Relationship. Affirmations and daily practice can go a long way to changing unhealthy conditioning, and for the Female Led Relationships, patriarchal conditioning.

Couple's therapist and bestselling author Terry Real is a member of the senior faculty at the Family Institute of Cambridge and Director of the Gender Relations program at the Meadows Institute in Arizona. Terry Real says, "We all live under patriarchy, which is a rigid dichotomy of gender roles. Traditionally, men are supposed to be strong and feel independent, unemotional, logical, and confident. Women are supposed to be expressive, nurturer, weak, and dependent. One of the things I say about those traditional gender roles is they don't make anybody happy and they don't make for intimacy."

He believes that in order to lead men and women into happiness and intimacy, they must be led out of patriarchy since they are old rules not built for intimacy and happiness. He says, "The essence of masculinity is contempt for the feminine. Misogyny and masculinity are flip sides of the same coin. What it means to be a "man" today is not to be a girl. Not be feminine. The contempt for the feminine is part of the patriarchal culture." This leads to more unhealthy relationships, which could be part of the reason why the divorce rate is at 50 percent.

What's worse is that the real origin of patriarchy is not really known. Patriarchy is associated with a set of ideas—a patriarchal ideology that acts to explain and justify this dominance and attributes it to inherent natural differences between men and women. If we truly analyze what men want, patriarchy also fails to fulfill these needs. In a recent study, men described the reason leading to their divorces and what they most value in a woman. From this, it was concluded that the goal of men is to reduce complexity in their lives and what men want most from women is to feel truly appreciated. It's all about simplicity and appreciation.

Female Led Relationships address both of these needs. A strong woman in charge helps to simplify things because she leads while the man follows. In addition, when a man worships and serves a woman correctly, he will feel appreciated and rewarded. Female Led Relationships are growing because they are congruent with the state of our existence.

With women leading, there is much more emphasis on communication and empathy. The world needs more communication in a digital world and not much brute strength. A man can begin to develop his intuitive, empathetic side with affirmations that focus on serving his woman. Not only does this place focus on his woman daily, but he also retains a goal and purpose in his life.

Conclusion

The Female Led Relationship is one of the most exciting adventures that you and your Queen will embark on. At the source of female led is obedience, discipline, and submission. Your role is to serve her and she must lead. You each have a responsibility in the relationship to take care of your part while coming together, communicating with love and respect for each other. Rules and boundaries help with day-to-day life, but no matter what experience you decide to explore, there must always be consent.

Modern life means there needs to be a modern relationship, and the Female Led Relationship is timely with female empowerment and the Future is Female, so you can be confident that your union helps both of you to evolve. Female led life has the ability to transform your relationship or marriage, and couples have reported more intimacy and connection. There are many different experiences to explore together, including female led sex, oral pleasure, chastity, cuckolding, consensual non-monogamy, spanking, BDSM, and discipline.

One of the challenges for men is to release past patriarchal conditioning, but with the help of daily affirmations of female worship, you can overcome this, which helps you to learn to accept your Queen as your supreme leader and Goddess. It is my hope that you both will experience the transformative effects of female led life and the *Love & Obey* movement that thousands of couples have worldwide.

www.ingramcontent.com/pod-product-compliance
Lightning Source LLC
Chambersburg PA
CBHW071944090426
42740CB00011B/1810